This collection first published in 2008 by
Express Newspapers
The Northern & Shell Building
10 Lower Thames Street
London EC3R 6EN

ISBN-13: 978-0-85079-349-9

Cover design and typesetting by Susie Bell

Printed and bound in Poland. Produced by Polskabook

DAILY EXPRESS

Forgotten Treasures
Volume III

Compiled by
William Hartston

The Daily Express

Contents

Introduction

'Poetry is all that is worth remembering in life'
William Hazlitt (1778–1830)

Less than two years have passed since a reader wrote to the *Daily Express* asking if we could identify a poem from a few lines that kept coming back to her. Our positive response to that enquiry resulted in a deluge of similar letters and the inauguration of the 'Forgotten Verse' column in the newspaper. Since then we have received some ten thousand letters and emails from people begging to be reunited with poems heard on their grannies' knees, or learnt at school, or shared with first loves, or sobbed over at funerals. And still they arrive by every post.

Putting together this third collection of *Forgotten Treasures*, I am struck by the astonishing breadth of readers' tastes. Spanning nearly four centuries and covering every aspect of life and human emotion, they offer a glimpse into the power of poetry to encapsulate all that is worth remembering. The many letters of thanks I have received after identifying lost fragments testify to the joy that can be felt when poetry brings back those lost memories.

William Hartston
January 2008

1.

Love

THE DOVE
by John Keats

I had a dove, and the sweet dove died;
And I have thought it died of grieving:
Oh, what could it grieve for? its feet were tied
With a silken thread of my own hands' weaving.
Sweet little red feet! Why should you die—
Why would you leave me, sweet bird! why?
You lived alone in the forest tree;
Why, pretty thing! would you not live with me?
I kiss'd you oft and gave you white peas;
Why not live sweetly, as in the green trees?

John Keats (1795–1821)
G Day of Chichester wrote in with a poignant memory of this verse about lost
love, written by John Keats: 'At the age of six, in 1929, my class started to
learn a poem at school about a dove that had died. A little girl in the class
used to cry and the teacher would let her stand outside the classroom until we
had finished.'

CUPID STUNG
by Thomas Moore

Cupid once upon a bed
Of roses laid his weary head;
Luckless urchin, not to see
Within the leaves a slumbering bee.
The bee awak'd – with anger wild
The bee awak'd, and stung the child.
Loud and piteous are his cries;
To Venus quick he runs, he flies;
'Oh, Mother! I am wounded through –
I die with pain – in sooth I do!
Stung by some little angry thing,
Some serpent on a tiny wing
A bee it was – or once, I know,
I heard a rustic call it so.'
Thus he spoke, and she the while
Heard him with a soothing smile;
Then said, 'My infant, if so much
Thou feel the little wild bee's touch,
How must the heart, ah, Cupid! be,
The hapless heart that's stung by thee!

Thomas Moore (1779–1852)
Thomas Moore was an Irish poet, songwriter and entertainer, who also impressed as a society figure in London and was appointed registrar to the admiralty in Bermuda. He is now best remembered as the writer of the lyrics to 'The Last Rose of Summer' and 'Believe Me If All Those Endearing Young Charms'. Jayne Woods requested this poem via email.

SORROWS OF WERTHER
by William Makepeace Thackeray

Werther had a love for Charlotte
Such as words could never utter;
Would you know how first he met her?
She was cutting bread and butter.

Charlotte was a married lady,
And a moral man was Werther,
And for all the wealth of Indies,
Would do nothing for to hurt her.

So he sighed and pined and ogled,
And his passion boiled and bubbled.
Till he blew his silly brains out,
And no more was by it troubled.

Charlotte, having seen his body
Borne before her on a shutter,
Like a well-conducted person,
Went on cutting bread and butter.

William Makepeace Thackeray (1811–63)
As the author of novels such as Vanity Fair *and* Pendennis, *William Thackeray was perhaps the second most highly reputed writer of the Victorian age, behind only Charles Dickens, yet his success as a novelist makes it easy to overlook his brilliance as a biting satirist and writer of humorous verse. Isobel Chambers requested this verse, and recalled only the lines 'blew his silly brains out' and 'went on cutting bread and butter'.*

TRIOLET
by Robert Bridges

All women born are so perverse
No man need boast their love possessing.
If naught seem better, nothing's worse:
All women born are so perverse.
From Adam's wife, that proved a curse,
Though God had made her for a blessing,
All women born are so perverse
No man need boast their love possessing.

Robert Bridges (1844–1930)
*A triolet is a poem that includes the same line three times. In this case,
unsurprisingly, that was the line that stuck in the memory of Joan Armitage
of Northampton, who first requested it. Robert Bridges was Poet Laureate
from 1913 until his death in 1930.*

MAIDEN EYES
by Gerald Griffin

You never bade me hope, 'tis true;
    I ask'd you not to swear:
But I look'd in those eyes of blue,
    And read a promise there.

The vow should bind, with maiden sighs
    That maiden lips have spoken:
But that which looks from maiden eyes
    Should last of all be broken.

Gerald Griffin (1803–40)
Gerald Griffin was an Irish novelist, poet, and playwright, who only found
true contentment after burning all his manuscripts and joining a religious
order where he could write in peace and, as he put it, be 'absorbed in the
modest project of rivalling Shakespeare'.
    Robert Chalmers from Durham requested this poem.

WHEN I SAW YOU LAST, ROSE
by Austin Dobson

When I saw you last, Rose,
You were only so high; –
How fast the time goes!

Like a bud ere it blows,
You just peeped at the sky,
When I saw you last, Rose!

Now your petals unclose,
Now your May-time is nigh; –
How fast the time goes!

And a life, – how it grows!
You were scarcely so shy,
When I saw you last, Rose!

In your bosom it shows
There's a guest on the sly;
(How fast the time goes!)

Is it Cupid? Who knows!
Yet you used not to sigh,
When I saw you last, Rose; –
How fast the time goes!

Austin Dobson (1840–1921)
Austin Dobson was a relatively undistinguished civil servant, but a successful part-time poet and biographer. His entire working life was spent at the Board of Trade, where he rose to the rank of principal in the harbour department, which evidently left him enough time to produce several volumes of splendidly witty poems as well as a number of well-researched biographies. Elizabeth Rose of West London requested this poem.

CUPID DROWNED
by Leigh Hunt

T'other day, as I was twining
Roses, for a crown to dine in,
What, of all things, 'mid the heap,
Should I light on, fast asleep,
But the little desperate elf,
The tiny traitor, Love, himself!
By the wings I picked him up
Like a bee, and in a cup
Of my wine I plunged and sank him,
Then what d'ye think I did? – I drank him.
Faith, I thought him dead. Not he!
There he lives with tenfold glee;
And now this moment with his wings
I feel him tickling my heartstrings.

Leigh Hunt (1784–1859)
James Henry Leigh Hunt was a friend of Byron and Shelley, each of whom
supported him through times of great personal poverty. His own verse displays
great wit, as well as high sincerity and good taste. His best-known poem is the
often-requested 'Abou Ben Adhem' (included in the first book of Forgotten
Treasures). *Gareth Jones of Liverpool requested this cheerfully witty*
love poem.

IF I HAD BUT TWO LITTLE WINGS
by Samuel Taylor Coleridge

If I had but two little wings
And were a little feathery bird,
To you I'd fly, my dear!
But thoughts like these are idle things
And I stay here.

But in my sleep to you I fly:
I'm always with you in my sleep!
The world is all one's own.
And then one wakes, and where am I?
All, all alone.

Samuel Taylor Coleridge (1772–1834)
Samuel Taylor Coleridge is generally regarded – alongside Wordsworth – as one of the founders of the English Romantic movement in poetry. His epic poem 'The Rime of the Ancient Mariner' is rightly regarded as his finest work, but as the above example shows, he could also write short verse. Emily Taylor of Gloucester requested this poem.

LA BELLE DAME SANS MERCI
by John Keats

O what can ail thee, knight-at-arms,
Alone and palely loitering?
The sedge has wither'd from the lake,
And no birds sing.

O what can ail thee, knight-at-arms!
So haggard and so woe-begone?
The squirrel's granary is full,
And the harvest's done.

I see a lily on thy brow
With anguish moist and fever dew,
And on thy cheeks a fading rose
Fast withereth too.

I met a lady in the meads,
Full beautiful – a faery's child,
Her hair was long, her foot was light,
And her eyes were wild.

I made a garland for her head,
And bracelets too, and fragrant zone;
She look'd at me as she did love,
And made sweet moan.

I set her on my pacing steed,
And nothing else saw all day long,
For sidelong would she lean, and sing
A faery's song.

She found me roots of relish sweet,
And honey wild, and manna dew
And sure in language strange she said—
'I love thee true.'

She took me to her elfin grot,
And there she wept, and sigh'd full sore,
And there I shut her wild wild eyes
With kisses four.

And there she lullèd me asleep,
And there I dream'd—ah! Woe betide!
The latest dream I ever dream'd
On the cold hill's side.

I saw pale kings and princes too,
Pale warriors, death-pale were they all;
They cried—'La Belle Dame sans Merci
Hath thee in thrall!'

I saw their starved lips in the gloam,
With horrid warning gapèd wide,
And I awoke and found me here,
On the cold hill's side.

And this is why I sojourn here,
Alone and palely loitering,
Though the sedge is wither'd from the lake,
And no birds sing.

John Keats is the perfect model of a tragic romantic poet, dying in Rome at the age of twenty-five, but leaving behind an impressive amount of great poetry. His last request was to be buried under a tombstone bearing no name, but the words, 'Here lies one whose name was writ in water.'

This is one of the best-known and saddest love poems in the English language and was requested by Michael Freeman from Colchester, who wrote: 'I remember struggling to learn it at school over half a century ago, and can't get further than "alone and palely loitering" these days. But I know it was a beautiful poem.'

WITH STRAWBERRIES
by William Ernest Henley

With strawberries we filled a tray,
And then we drove away, away
Along the links beside the sea,
Where wave and wind were light and free,
And August felt as fresh as May.

And where the springy turf was gay
With thyme and balm and many a spray
Of wild roses, you tempted me
With strawberries.

A shadowy sail, silent and gray,
Stole like a ghost across the bay;
But none could hear me ask my fee,
And none could know what came to be.
Can sweethearts *all* their thirst allay
With strawberries?

William Ernest Henley (1849–1903)
*William Ernest Henley was an English poet, best remembered for the closing
lines of his inspiring verse 'Invictus': 'I am the master of my fate: I am the
captain of my soul'. The charming poem above was requested by Maggie
Jones in an email, who said she recalled it when she was packing some
strawberries for a family afternoon in the sun.*

CHILD, CHILD
by Sara Teasdale

Child, child, love while you can
The voice and the eyes and the soul of a man,
Never fear though it break your heart –
Out of the wound new joy will start;
Only love proudly and gladly and well
Though love be heaven or love be hell.

Child, child, love while you may,
For life is short as a happy day;
Never fear the thing you feel –
Only by love is life made real;
Love, for the deadly sins are seven,
Only through love will you enter heaven.

Sara Teasdale (1884–1933)
Sara Teasdale was an American poet whose joyous verse was the complete opposite of her own tragic life. Problems with health and romance led her to take her own life with an overdose of sleeping pills at the age of forty-eight.

THE TRUE BEAUTY
by Thomas Carew

He that loves a rosy cheek
Or a coral lip admires,
Or from star-like eyes doth seek
Fuel to maintain his fires;
As old Time makes these decay,
So his flames must waste away.

But a smooth and steadfast mind,
Gentle thoughts, and calm desires,
Hearts with equal love combined,
Kindle never-dying fires:—
Where these are not, I despise
Lovely cheeks or lips or eyes.

Thomas Carew (1595–1639?)
Thomas Carew was a poet and courtier who served as 'taster-in-ordinary' to King Charles I. Emily Morgan requested this poem via an e-mail.

SONNET 116
by William Shakespeare

Let me not to the marriage of true minds
Admit impediments. Love is not love
Which alters when it alteration finds,
Or bends with the remover to remove:
O no! it is an ever-fixed mark
That looks on tempests and is never shaken;
It is the star to every wandering bark,
Whose worth's unknown, although his height be taken.
Love's not Time's fool, though rosy lips and cheeks
Within his bending sickle's compass come:
Love alters not with his brief hours and weeks,
But bears it out even to the edge of doom.
If this be error and upon me proved,
I never writ, nor no man ever loved.

William Shakespeare (1564–1616)
The plays of William Shakespeare are so outstanding that his sonnets – 154 of them – are often neglected by comparison; yet they contain some of the Bard's finest writing. This one was requested by ninety-four-year-old WL Wardle of Bolton who saw it as 'expressing the meaning of Easter – i.e. love – in a wonderful way'.

THERE IS A LADY SWEET AND KIND
by Barnabe Googe

There is a Lady sweet and kind,
Was never face so pleased my mind;
I did but see her passing by,
And yet I love her till I die.

Her gesture, motion, and her smiles,
Her wit her voice my heart beguiles,
Beguiles my heart, I know not why,
And yet I love her till I die.

Cupid is wingèd and doth range,
Her country so my love doth change:
But change she earth, or change she sky,
Yet will I love her till I die.

Barnabe Googe (1540–94)
As David Holmes reminded us when he wrote from New South Wales, the former Australian Prime Minister, Sir Robert Menzies, quoted this poem when the Queen visited Australia in the 1950s. The verse dates back to the first Queen Elizabeth but there is some doubt over who wrote it. The general opinion seems to be that it was written by Barnabe Googe.

WHO IS SILVIA?
by William Shakespeare

Who is Silvia? what is she,
That all our swains commend her?
Holy, fair, and wise is she;
The heaven such grace did lend her,
That she might admirèd be.

Is she kind as she is fair?
For beauty lives with kindness.
Love doth to her eyes repair,
To help him of his blindness,
And, being help'd, inhabits there.

Then to Silvia let us sing,
That Silvia is excelling;
She excels each mortal thing
Upon the dull earth dwelling:
To her let us garlands bring.

Eleanor McHugh of High Wycombe, Bucks, asked for this poem, which she learnt at school in the 1930s and can now only remember parts of. 'I am now eight-five-plus and my memory isn't what it used to be', she says.

The poem is a song found in Shakespeare's Two Gentlemen of Verona. *There is a beautiful musical setting of it by Schubert.*

TO ALTHEA, FROM PRISON
by Richard Lovelace

When Love with unconfinèd wings
    Hovers within my gates,
And my divine Althea brings
    To whisper at the grates;
When I lie tangled in her hair
    And fetter'd to her eye,
The birds that wanton in the air,
    Know no such liberty.

When flowing cups run swiftly round
    With no allaying Thames,
Our careless heads with roses bound,
    Our hearts with loyal flames;
When thirsty grief in wine we steep,
When healths and draughts go free—
    Fishes that tipple in the deep
    Know no such liberty.

When, like committed linnets, I
    With shriller throat shall sing
The sweetness, mercy, majesty,
    And glories of my King;
When I shall voice aloud how good
    He is, how great should be,
Enlargèd winds that curl the flood,
    Know no such liberty.

Stone walls do not a prison make,
Nor iron bars a cage;
Minds innocent and quiet take
That for an hermitage;
If I have freedom in my love
And in my soul am free,
Angels alone, that soar above,
Enjoy such liberty.

Richard Lovelace (1618–57)
*The opening lines of the last verse of this poem are frequently quoted, though
few realise that they come from a love poem. Lovelace wrote it while
imprisoned for supporting the Royalist cause in the time of Oliver Cromwell.*

*Mrs V Goodwin from Morecambe, who was perplexed by a single line,
first requested this: 'The only snippet of this poem that I remember is
"[something] do not a prison make, nor iron bars a cage".'*

BE MY MISTRESS SHORT OR TALL
by Robert Herrick

Be my mistress short or tall,
And distorted therewithall,
Be she likewise one of those,
That an acre hath of nose,
Be her teeth ill hung or set,
And her grinders black as jet,
Be her cheeks so shallow too,
As to show her tongue wag through,
Hath she thin hair, hath she none,
She's to me a paragon.

Robert Herrick (1591–1674)
This is a delightfully unusual verse by the seventeenth-century poet Robert Herrick, much of whose work wallows in romantic idealisim, but this one is amusing and down to earth.

Henry Richards of Tonbridge, Kent, remembered the general 'love her for all her faults' message, and the final word 'paragon'.

2.

Nature

THE WORLD IS TOO MUCH WITH US
by William Wordsworth

The world is too much with us; late and soon,
Getting and spending, we lay waste our powers;
Little we see in Nature that is ours;
We have given our hearts away, a sordid boon!
This sea, that bares her bosom to the moon,
The winds that will be howling at all hours,
And are up-gathered now like sleeping flowers
For this, for everything, we are out of tune;
It moves us not. —Great God! I'd rather be
A pagan, suckled in a creed outworn,
So might I, standing on this pleasant lea,
Have glimpses that would make me less forlorn;
Have sight of Proteus rising from the sea;
Or hear old Triton blow his wreathed horn.

William Wordsworth (1770–1850)
*William Wordsworth was one of the great English romantic poets and served
as Poet Laureate from 1843 until his death. The above sonnet tells us all not
to be distracted by material goods and lose sight of the simple life and beauties
of the world.*

CONSIDER THE LILIES OF THE FIELD
by Christina Rossetti

Flowers preach to us if we will hear:-
The rose saith in the dewy morn:
I am most fair;
Yet all my loveliness is born
Upon a thorn.
The poppy saith amid the corn:
Let but my scarlet head appear
And I am held in scorn;
Yet juice of subtle virtue lies
Within my cup of curious dyes.
The lilies say: Behold how we
Preach without words of purity.
The violets whisper from the shade
Which their own leaves have made:
Men scent our fragrance on the air,
Yet take no heed
Of humble lessons we would read.
But not alone the fairest flowers:
The merest grass
Along the roadside where we pass,
Lichen and moss and sturdy weed,
Tell of His love who sends the dew,
The rain and sunshine too,
To nourish one small seed.

Christina Rossetti (1830–94)
Carol Tasker of Tetney, Lincs, asked for the verse that takes its title from
Christ's Sermon on the Mount, as recorded in Chapter 6 of St Matthew's
Gospel: 'Consider the lilies of the field, how they grow; they toil not, neither do
they spin: And yet I say unto you, That even Solomon in all his glory was not
arrayed like one of these.'

LOVELIEST OF TREES, THE CHERRY NOW
by A E Housman

Loveliest of trees, the cherry now
Is hung with bloom along the bough,
And stands about the woodland ride
Wearing white for Eastertide.

Now, of my threescore years and ten,
Twenty will not come again,
And take from seventy springs a score,
It only leaves me fifty more.

And since to look at things in bloom
Fifty springs are little room,
About the woodlands I will go
To see the cherry hung with snow.

A E Housman (1859–1936)
Julia Searle from southeast London requested this poem; she remembered learning it in high school in Sunbury-upon-Thames thirty-five years ago.

FROM COWSLIPS AND KINGCUPS
by Charlotte Druitt Cole

Hand in hand they dance in a row
Hither and thither, and to and fro,
Flip! flap! flop! and away they go –
Fluttering creatures as white as snow.

Like restive horses they caper and prance;
Like fairy-tale witches they wildly dance;
Rounded in front, hollow behind,
They shiver and skip in the merry March wind.

One I saw dancing excitedly,
Struggling so wildly she was free,
Then, leaving pegs and clothes-line behind her.
I saw her gleam, like a sail in the sun,
Flipping and flapping, and flopping for fun.

Nobody knows where she now can be,
Hid in a ditch, or drowned in the sea.
She was my handkerchief not long ago,
But she'll never come back to my pocket, I know.

Charlotte Druitt Cole (dates unknown)
*Charlotte Druitt Cole was a popular writer of children's verse in the early
years of the twentieth century. Christina Melling from Nelson, Lancs, wrote
in search of this poem for an old friend who had not seen it since she was six.*

ELLAN VANNIN
by Eliza Craven Green

When the summer day is over
And the busy cares have flown,
Then I sit beneath the starlight
With a weary heart. alone,
And there rises like a vision,
Sparkling bright in nature's glee,
My own dear Ellan Vannin
With its green hills by the sea.

Then I hear the wavelets murmur
As they kiss the fairy shore,
Then beneath the em'rald waters
Sings the mermaid as of yore,
And the fair Isle shines with beauty
As in youth it dawned on me,
My own dear Ellan Vannin
With its green hills by the sea.

Then mem'ries sweet and tender
Come like music's plaintive flow,
Of someone in Ellan Vannin
That lov'd me long ago,
So I give with tears and blessings,
And my fondest thoughts to thee,
My own dear Ellan Vannin
With its green hills by the sea.

Eliza Craven Green (dates unknown)
This is the only poem in this collection that began with a request for a song by the BeeGees. Annie Gray of Hawick wrote: 'I have a CD of the BeeGees singing a haunting melody called "Ellan Vannin". A friend tells me the BeeGees wrote the words, but I feel sure it is an old poem put to music.'

'Ellan Vannin', which is the Manx name for the Isle of Man, was written by Eliza Craven Green long before the BeeGees were thought of – in 1854 to be exact. But the BeeGees amended the words for their own recording, made to raise money for Isle of Man charities. The lines above are the original verse.

TO A CHILD FIVE YEARS OLD
by Nathaniel Cotton

Fairest flower, all flowers excelling,
  Which in Eden's garden grew;
Flowers of Eve's embowered dwelling
  Are, my fair one, types of you.

Mark, my Polly, how the roses
  Emulate thy damask cheek;
How the bud its sweets discloses—
  Buds thy opening bloom bespeak.

Lilies are, by plain direction,
  Emblems of a double kind;
Emblems of thy fair complexion,
  Emblems of thy fairer mind.

But, dear girl, both flowers and beauty
  Blossom, fade, and die away;
Then pursue good sense and duty,
  Evergreens that ne'er decay.

Nathaniel Cotton (1707–88)
Apart from being a poet, Nathaniel Cotton was a distinguished surgeon, with
a particular interest in the treatment of mental illnesses. Mrs Bennison of
North Yorkshire found the first verse above on a bookmark, which she told us
was a gift from her husband many years ago.

MINE HOST OF 'THE GOLDEN APPLE'
by Thomas Westwood

A goodly host one day was mine,
A Golden Apple his only sign,
That hung from a long branch, ripe and fine.
My host was the bountiful apple tree;
He gave me shelter and nourished me
With the best of fare, all fresh and free.

And light-winged guests came not a few,
To his leafy inn, and sipped the dew,
And sang their best songs ere they flew.

I slept at night, on a downy bed
Of moss, and my Host benignly spread
His own cool shadow over my head.
When I asked what reckoning there might be,
He shook his broad boughs cheerily:—
A blessing be thine, green Apple tree!

Thomas Westwood (1814–88)
*Thomas Westwood was a businessman, poet, and keen angler, with a
particular interest in books on fishing. Pat Young requested this poem: 'My
mother-in-law, Norah Young, remembers one line of a poem from her youth,
many years ago. It refers to "my host the golden apple". I don't know if this is
sufficient info, but I hope you can help.'*

FAIRY SONG
by John Keats

Shed no tear! oh, shed no tear!
The flower will bloom another year.
Weep no more! oh, weep no more!
Young buds sleep in the root's white core.
Dry your eyes! oh, dry your eyes!
For I was taught in Paradise
To ease my breast of melodies,—
Shed no tear.

Overhead! look overhead!
'Mong the blossoms white and red—
Look up, look up! I flutter now
On this fresh pomegranate bough.
See me! 'tis this silvery bill
Ever cures the good man's ill.
Shed no tear! oh, shed no tear!
The flower will bloom another year.
Adieu, adieu —I fly—adieu!
I vanish in the heaven's blue,—
Adieu, adieu!

Emily Carroll of Cardiff requested this verse, and told us that she read it at school over seventy years ago and found it very moving.

3.

Wind and Rain

WHO HAS SEEN THE WIND?
by Christina Rossetti

Who has seen the wind?
Neither I nor you:
But when the leaves hang trembling
The wind is passing thro'.

Who has seen the wind?
Neither you nor I:
But when the trees bow down their heads
The wind is passing by.

This is a typically delicate short verse by Christina Rossetti, who was arguably the best female British poet of the late nineteenth century.
Pat Lamb of Prestwich first requested this poem.

WINDY NIGHTS
by Robert Louis Stevenson

Whenever the moon and stars are set,
Whenever the wind is high,
All night long in the dark and wet,
A man goes riding by.
Late in the night when the fires are out,
Why does he gallop and gallop about?

Whenever the trees are crying aloud,
And ships are tossed at sea,
By, on the highway, low and loud,
By at the gallop goes he.
By at the gallop he goes, and then
By he comes back at the gallop again.

Robert Louis Stevenson (1850–94)
Even if Robert Louis Stevenson had not written such classics as Treasure
Island *and* Dr Jekyll and Mr Hyde, *he would have earned a high literary
reputation for his children's poetry. This verse is from his marvelous
collection,* A Child's Garden Of Verses, *and was requested by L Hardiman-
Hunt of Stansted, Essex who recalled it as 'a poem or song our teacher used to
sing to us at infant school.'*

WHEN THE WIND IS IN THE EAST
Anonymous

When the wind is in the east,
'Tis neither good for man nor beast;
When the wind is in the north,
The skilful fisher goes not forth;
When the wind is in the south,
It blows the bait in the fishes' mouth;
When the wind is in the west,
Then 'tis at the very best.

Nobody knows the origin of this old weather proverb, which dates back at least to the 1840s when it appeared in Halliwell's Nursery Rhymes of England.

Mrs ME Canner of Ashby de la Zouch in Leicestershire requested it: 'Help please. This is driving me mad. I know "When the wind is in the east it's neither fit for man nor beast", and I know the lines for west and south, but what the dickens happens when the wind is in the north? None of my elderly friends can remember.'

THE DAWN WIND
by Rudyard Kipling

At two o'clock in the morning, if you open your window and listen,
  You will hear the feet of the Wind that is going to call the sun.
And the trees in the shadow rustle and the trees in the moonlight glisten,
  And though it is deep, dark night, you feel that the night is done.

So do the cows in the field. They graze for an hour and lie down,
  Dozing and chewing the cud; or a bird in the ivy wakes,
Chirrups one note and is still, and the restless Wind strays on,
  Fidgeting far down the road, till, softly, the darkness breaks.

Back comes the Wind full strength with a blow like an angel's wing,
  Gentle but waking the world, as he shouts: 'The Sun! The Sun!'
And the light floods over the fields and the birds begin to sing,
  And the Wind dies down in the grass. It is day and his work is done.

So when the world is asleep, and there seems no hope of her waking
  Out of some long, bad dream that makes her mutter and moan,
Suddenly, all men arise to the noise of fetters breaking,
  And every one smiles at his neighbour and tells him his soul is his own!

Rudyard Kipling (1865–1936)
Famed for The Jungle Book, *the* Just So Stories, *and a good deal of stirring*
patriotic and militaristic verse, Rudyard Kipling could also write with great
effect about nature.
    Mrs B Grant from Newport, Isle of Wight, remembered the opening lines
from her schooldays during the Second World War.

WIND
by Amy Lowell

He shouts in the sails of the ships at sea,
He steals the down from the honeybee,
He makes the forest trees rustle and sing,
He twirls my kite till it breaks its string.
Laughing, dancing, sunny wind,
Whistling, howling, rainy wind,
North, South, East and West,
Each is the wind I like the best.

He calls up the fog and hides the hills,
He whirls the wings of the great windmills,
The weathercocks love him and turn to discover
His whereabouts – but he's gone, the rover!
Laughing, dancing, sunny wind,
Whistling, howling, rainy wind,
North, South, East and West,
Each is the wind I like the best.

The pine trees toss him their cones with glee,
The flowers bend low in courtesy,
Each wave flings up a shower of pearls,
The flag in front of the school unfurls.
Laughing, dancing, sunny wind,
Whistling, howling, rainy wind,
North, South, East and West,
Each is the wind I like the best.

Amy Lowell (1874–1925)
This is another windy poem by someone with good family connections to write
about atmospheric events: Amy Lowell was the sister of the astronomer
Percival Lowell, the man who discovered the planet Pluto.

FALLING SNOW
Anonymous

See the pretty snowflakes
Falling from the sky;
On the wall and housetops
Soft and thick they lie.

On the window ledges,
On the branches bare;
Now how fast they gather,
Filling all the air.

Look into the garden,
Where the grass was green;
Covered by the snowflakes,
Not a blade is seen.

Now the bare black bushes
All look soft and white,
Every twig is laden,
What a pretty sight!

Mrs G Dillon of Bicester – who recalled the opening lines from this verse, which her grandmother used to recite to her – requested this.

THE HAG
by Robert Herrick

The hag is astride
This night for to ride,
The devil and she together;
Through thick and through thin,
Now out and then in,
Though ne'er so foul be the weather.

A thorn or a burr
She takes for a spur,
With a lash of a bramble she rides now;
Through brakes and through briars,
O'er ditches and mires,
She follows the spirit that guides now.

No beast for his food
Dare now range the wood,
But hush'd in his lair he lies lurking;
While mischiefs, by these,
On land and on seas,
At noon of night are a-working.

The storm will arise
And trouble the skies;
This night, and more for the wonder,
The ghost from the tomb
Affrighted shall come,
Call'd out by the clap of the thunder.

Robert Herrick is best known for his sentimental and romantic verses, but this poem is very different.

Mrs Oakman of Royston, Herts, wrote: 'I was eleven when I went to senior school some fifty years ago. We had a small but very strict teacher. The first poem we learnt began: "The witch is astride, this night for to ride, the devil and she together" which made my friend and me burst out laughing and we couldn't tell the teacher why.' We were happy to provide the full poem, correcting Mrs Oakham's 'witch' to a hag.

THE RAINBOW
by Thomas Campbell

Triumphal arch, that fills the sky
When storms prepare to part,
I ask not proud Philosophy
To teach me what thou art.

Still seem, as to my childhood's sight,
A midway station given,
For happy spirits to alight,
Betwixt the earth and heaven.

Thomas Campbell (1777–1844)
*Thomas Campbell was a Scottish poet, who is also celebrated as one of the
founders of London University. This verse was requested in an e-mail from
'Anne' of Aberdeen.*

THE RAINBOW FAIRIES
by Lizzie M Hadley

Two little clouds one summer's day,
Went flying through the sky.
They went so fast they bumped their heads,
And both began to cry.
Old Father Sun looked out and said,
'Oh, never mind, my dears,
I'll send my little fairy folk
To dry your falling tears.'
One fairy came in violet,
And one in indigo,
In blue, green, yellow, orange, red, –
They made a pretty row.
They wiped the cloud tears all away,
And then, from out the sky,
Upon a line of sunbeams made,
They hung their gowns to dry.

Lizzie M Hadley (dates unknown)
Lizzie M Hadley was a writer of children's verse, who flourished around the beginning of the twentieth century.
    This verse brought back memories for Sarah Wilson from the Vale of Glamorgan: 'I remember my grandmother teaching me a poem when I was a little girl many years ago, which helped me win top prize in my class at Cranford Junior School.'

THE RAINY DAY
by Henry Wadsworth Longfellow

The day is cold, and dark, and dreary;
It rains, and the wind is never weary;
The vine still clings to the mouldering wall,
But at every gust the dead leaves fall,
And the day is dark and dreary.

My life is cold, and dark, and dreary;
It rains, and the wind is never weary;
My thoughts still cling to the mouldering past,
But the hopes of youth fall thick in the blast,
And the days are dark and dreary.

Be still, sad heart! and cease repining;
Behind the clouds is the sun still shining;
Thy fate is the common fate of all,
Into each life some rain must fall,
Some days must be dark and dreary.

Henry Wadsworth Longfellow (1807–82)
The year 2007 saw the bicentenary of the birth of Henry Wadsworth Longfellow, who remains the only American poet celebrated with a bust in Poets' Corner at Westminster Abbey.

A spate of bad weather, rather than bicentenary celebrations, brought the above poem back into the memory of Graham Bond, who told us in an email that he had learnt it at school but could now only remember 'the day is dark and dreary' at the end of each verse.

4.

Seas and Rivers

THE TIDE RIVER (from *The Water Babies*)
by Charles Kingsley

Clear and cool, clear and cool,
By laughing shallow, and dreaming pool;
Cool and clear, cool and clear,
By shining shingle, and foaming wear;
Under the crag where the ouzel sings,
And the ivied wall where the church-bell rings,
Undefiled, for the undefiled;
Play by me, bathe in me, mother and child.

Dank and foul, dank and foul,
By the smoky town in its murky cowl;
Foul and dank, foul and dank,
By wharf and sewer and slimy bank;
Darker and darker the farther I go,
Baser and baser the richer I grow;
Who dare sport with the sin-defiled?
Shrink from me, turn from me, mother and child.

Strong and free, strong and free,
The floodgates are open, away to the sea.
Free and strong, free and strong,
Cleansing my streams as I hurry along
To the golden sands, and the leaping bar,
And the taintless tide that awaits me afar,
As I lose myself in the infinite main,
Like a soul that has sinned and is pardoned again.
Undefiled, for the undefiled;
Play by me, bathe in me, mother and child.

Charles Kingsley (1819–75)
Charles Kingsley was a rector, poet, writer, and Professor of Modern History at Cambridge, and is best known now for his novels Westward Ho! *and* The Water Babies. *The above poem comes from the end of the first chapter of* The Water Babies *and was requested by Mrs A S Silva of Southall, Middlesex.*

THE MEETING OF THE WATERS
by Thomas Moore

There is not in the wide world a valley so sweet
As that vale in whose bosom the bright waters meet;
Oh the last rays of feeling and life must depart,
Ere the bloom of that valley shall fade from my heart.

Yet it was not that nature had shed o'er the scene
Her purest of crystal and brightest of green;
'Twas not her soft magic of streamlet or hill,
Oh! no – 'twas something more exquisite still.

'Twas that friends, the belov'd of my bosom, were near,
Who made every scene of enchantment more dear,
And who felt how the best charms of nature improve,
When we see them reflected from looks that we love.

Sweet vale of Avoca! how calm could I rest
In thy bosom of shade, with the friends I love best
Where the storms that we feel in this cold world would cease
And our hearts, like thy waters, be mingled in peace.

The Avoca is a river in County Wicklow, Ireland, which includes a point known as The Meeting of the Waters where the Avonmore (which means 'big river') meets the Avonbeg ('little river'). Poems such as this, which has also been set as a song, show why Thomas Moore has been considered Ireland's National Poet.

THE FULL SEA ROLLS AND THUNDERS
by William Ernest Henley

The full sea rolls and thunders
In glory and in glee.
O, bury me not in the senseless earth
But in the living sea!

Ay, bury me where it surges
A thousand miles from shore,
And in its brotherly unrest
I'll range for evermore.

This poem brought back wartime memories for John Duck, as he explained in an email: 'When I was at school during the war, we were tasked with learning poems and reciting them to pass the time while we were sitting in the air raid shelter. During an alert, one poem I recall went "The full sea rolls and thunders in glory and in glee, Oh bury me not in the (something) earth but in the living sea". I have tried to find it and the poet without success. Can you help?'

AFTON WATER
by Robert Burns

Flow gently, sweet Afton, among thy green braes!
Flow gently, I'll sing thee a song in thy praise;
My Mary's asleep by thy murmuring stream,
Flow gently, sweet Afton, disturb not her dream.

Thou stock-dove, whose echo resounds thro' the glen,
Ye wild whistling blackbirds in yon thorny den,
Thou green-crested lapwing, thy screaming forbear,
I charge you disturb not my slumbering fair.

How lofty, sweet Afton, thy neighbouring hills,
Far mark'd with the courses of clear winding rills;
There daily I wander as noon rises high,
My flocks and my Mary's sweet cot in my eye.

How pleasant thy banks and green valleys below,
Where wild in the woodlands the primroses blow;
There oft, as mild Ev'ning sweeps over the lea,
The sweet-scented birk shades my Mary and me.

Thy crystal stream, Afton, how lovely it glides,
And winds by the cot where my Mary resides,
How wanton thy waters her snowy feet lave,
As gathering sweet flowrets she stems thy clear wave.

Flow gently, sweet Afton, among thy green braes,
Flow gently, sweet river, the theme of my lays;
My Mary's asleep by thy murmuring stream,
Flow gently, sweet Afton, disturb not her dream.

Robert Burns (1721–84)
Afton Water, whose joys are extolled in this poem by Robert Burns, is a small river in Ayrshire. Unusually, its inclusion in this selection was inspired by a pack of cigarettes, as Edd Pearson explained when he wrote from Ormesby, Middlesborough: 'When I was in the army in Cyprus in the late 50s, we were able to get an issue of cigarettes called Passing Cloud. On the tin that contained them there was a country scene and a verse of a poem beginning, "Flow gently sweet Afton among thy green glades". Where is the sweet Afton? Who wrote it?'

TWILIGHT AT SEA
by Amelia Welby

The twilight hours, like birds, flew by,
As lightly and as free,
Ten thousand stars were in the sky,
Ten thousand on the sea;
For every wave, with dimpled face,
That leaped upon the air,
Had caught a star in its embrace,
And held it trembling there.

Amelia Welby (1891–52)
Amelia Welby lived in Baltimore in the United States and had her first poems
published when she was just twelve years old. This verse was requested by
Emily Taylor of Halifax.

WHERE THE BOATS GO
by Robert Louis Stevenson

Dark brown is the river.
Golden is the sand.
It flows along for ever,
With trees on either hand.

Green leaves a-floating,
Castles of the foam,
Boats of mine a-boating—
Where will all come home?

On goes the river
And out past the mill,
Away down the valley,
Away down the hill.

Away down the river,
A hundred miles or more,
Other little children
Shall bring my boats ashore.

This is another poem from Stevenson's A Child's Garden Of Verses And Underwoods *and was requested by Barbara Holbrook from the Isle of Wight: 'I have a head full of old poems from my childhood, but have forgotten several lines of a particular favourite. It begins "Dark brown is the river, golden is the sand" and ends, "Other little children will bring my boats ashore". Can you complete it for me?'*

TWENTY FROGGIES WENT TO SCHOOL
Anonymous

Twenty froggies went to school, down beside a rushy pool,
Twenty little coats of green, twenty vests all white and clean.
'We must be in time', said they; 'First we study, then we play;
That is how we keep the rule, when we froggies go to school.'

Master Froggy, grave and stern, called the classes in their turn,
Taught them how to nobly strive; likewise how to leap and dive;
From his seat upon a log, showed them how to say 'Kerchog!'
Also how to dodge a blow from the sticks which bad boys throw.

Twenty froggies grew up fast, big frogs they became at last;
Not one dunce among the lot; not one lesson they forgot;
Polished to a high degree, as each froggy ought to be,
Now they sit on other logs, teaching other little frogs.

This verse was a long lost memory for Christine Pearson of Bradford. 'My magical time as a child was when my mum would say a lovely poem to me, when I was so happy playing with my brothers and sisters,' she writes. 'Now I have four children and nine grandchildren and I can hardly remember the poem she told me. It began "Twenty froggies went to school".'

After this was published in the Daily Express *we received a letter from a schoolteacher in Russia saying she had given it to her class as a translation exercise. Now hands up all who know the Russian for 'Kerchog!'*

5.

Animals

SEA-GULLS
by Norah M Holland

Where the dark green hollows lift
Into crests of snow,
Wheeling, flashing, floating by,
White against the stormy sky,
With exultant call and cry
Swift the sea-gulls go.

Fearless, vagabond and free,
Children of the spray,
Spirits of old mariners
Drifting down the restless years—
Drake's and Hawkins' buccaneers,
So do sea-men say.

Watching, guarding, sailing still
Round the shores they knew,
Where the cliffs of Devon rise
Red against the sullen skies,
(Dearer far than Paradise)
'Mid the tossing blue.

Not for them the heavenly song;
Sweeter still they find
Than those angels, row on row,
Thunder of the bursting snow
Seething on the rocks below,
Singing of the wind.

Fairer than the streets of gold
Those wild fields of foam,
Where the horses of the sea
Stamp and whinny ceaselessly,
Warding from all enemy
Shores they once called home.

So the sea-gulls call and cry
'Neath the cliffs to-day,
Spirits of old mariners
Drifting down the restless years—
Drake's and Hawkins' buccaneers—
So do sea-men say!

Norah M Holland (1876–1925)
Norah Mary Holland was a Canadian with Irish ancestry and was a cousin of the poet William Butler Yeats.

Barbara Livings of St Albans wrote in: 'In the early 30s, I learnt a poem called "Sea-gulls" by Norah Holland. Unfortunately, all I can remember now are the words "wheeling, flashing, floating by". I lived in Southend-on-Sea, so this poem was very apt.'

TRUE ROYALTY
by Rudyard Kipling

There was never a Queen like Balkis,
From here to the wide world's end;
But Balkis talked to a butterfly
As you would talk to a friend.

There was never a King like Solomon,
Not since the world began;
But Solomon talked to a butterfly
As a man would talk to a man.

She was Queen of Sabaea –
And he was Asia's Lord –
But they both of 'em talked to butterflies
When they took their walks abroad!

This verse, requested by Margaret Carter of Cheltenham, comes from one of Kipling's Just So Stories *called 'The Butterfly That Stamped', but the verse has also appeared separately under the title given above.*

THE BUTTERFLY AND THE BEE
by William Lisle Bowles

Methought I heard a butterfly
  Say to a labouring bee:
'Thou hast no colours of the sky
  On painted wings like me.'

'Poor child of vanity! those dyes,
  And colours bright and rare,'
With mild reproof, the bee replies,
  'Are all beneath my care.'

'Content I toil from morn to eve,
  And scorning idleness,
To tribes of gaudy sloth I leave
  The vanity of dress.'

William Lisle Bowles (1762–1850)
First a classicist, then a vicar, and in 1818 chaplain to the Prince Regent,
William Lisle Bowles was described by contemporaries as an amiable but
rather eccentric man. His poetry, though much admired during his lifetime, is
now little known, though full of tenderness and grace. Margaret Price of
Manchester requested this verse, and recalled a teacher who used to refer to
over-dressed girls as 'gaudy sloths'.

THE KITTEN AND THE FALLING LEAVES
by William Wordsworth

That way look, my infant, lo!
What a pretty baby-show!
Eddying round and round they sink,
Softly, slowly, one might think.
From the motions that are made,
Every little leaf conveyed.
Sylph or Faery hither tending
To this lower world descending.
Each invisible and mute,
In his wavering parachute.

See the kitten on the wall
Sporting with the leaves that fall,
Withered leaves ... one ... two ... and three,
From the lofty elder-tree!
Through the calm and frosty air
Of this morning bright and fair.
But the kitten, how she starts,
Crouches, stretches, paws, and darts!
First at one, and then its fellow,
Just as light and just as yellow.

There are many now – now one
Now they stop and there are none:
What intenseness of desire
In her upward eye of fire!
With a tiger-leap half-way
Now she meets the coming prey,
Lets it go as fast, and then;
Has it in her power again.
Now she works with three or four,
Like an Indian conjuror;

Quick as he in feats of art,
Far beyond in joy of heart.
Where her antics played in the eye,
Of a thousand standers-by,
Clapping hands with shout and stare,
What would little Tabby care
For the plaudits of the crowd?
Over happy to be proud,
Over wealthy in the treasure
Of her exceeding pleasure.

This is the opening section of a longer poem by Wordsworth, containing all the parts most often quoted by cat lovers. Michael Browne of Reading requested it.

THE SNAIL
Anonymous

All along the garden wall, silvery and bright,
There's a line where a snail took a walk last night.
He came from the rockery for something to eat,
And those would be his footsteps if a snail had feet.

Have you ever seen a snail, going for a walk
With his house on his back and his eyes on stalks?
Well, when he has finished he rolls them in his head
And goes inside his tiny house, and tucks himself in bed.

We were set on this snail trail by Jean Macdonald of Sunderland who wrote:
'Some sixty years ago, I used to visit my grandfather every Sunday and it was
a standard request for me to stand on a stool and recite "The Snail",
beginning "All along the garden wall, silvery and white".'

HARK, HARK, THE DOGS DO BARK
Anonymous

Hark hark the dogs do bark
The beggars are coming to town
Some in rags and some in jags,
And one in a velvet gown.

This short verse, requested by Frank Evans of Enderby, Leicester, is an extremely old one with a long history. Some say it dates back to the thirteenth century, when barking dogs warned villagers of approaching strangers who might be carrying bubonic plague. Another explanation dates the verse back to the sixteenth century and the dissolution of the monasteries, likening the looting forces of Henry VIII to beggars and the 'one in a velvet gown' representing Thomas Cromwell. The 'jags' in the third line, incidentally, are garments with a slash or slit exposing material of a different colour.

THE THRUSH'S NEST
by John Clare

Within a thick and spreading hawthorn bush,
  That overhung a molehill large and round,
I heard from morn to morn a merry thrush
Sing hymns to sunrise, and I drank the sound
  With joy; and often, an intruding guest,
  I watched her secret toils from day to day –
How true she warped the moss to form a nest,
  And modelled it within with wood and clay;
And by and by, like heath-bells gilt with dew,
There lay her shining eggs, as bright as flowers,
  Ink-spotted-over shells of greeny blue;
  And there I witnessed in the sunny hours
A brood of nature's minstrels chirp and fly,
Glad as the sunshine and the laughing sky.

John Clare (1793–1864)
John Clare was known as 'the Northamptonshire Peasant poet' because of his humble origins. He was removed from his school at the age of seven so that he could tend the sheep and geese on the farm where his father worked. He later attended school in the evenings, and his talent for writing poetry – often in a Northamptonshire dialect – emerged.

  His erratic, and sometimes violent, behaviour meant he was confined to various mental asylums, which curiously enough is where he wrote much of his best work.

THE ROBIN
by Sir Lawrence Alma-Tadema

When father takes his spade to dig
then Robin comes along;
And sits upon a little twig
And sings a little song.

Or, if the trees are rather far,
He does not stay alone,
But comes up close to where we are
And bobs upon a stone.

Sir Lawrence Alma-Tadema (1836–1912)

Lawrence Alma-Tadema was a Dutch artist who moved to Britain in 1870. He was knighted in 1899 and awarded the Order of Merit in 1905. Though far better known as a painter, especially for his depictions of life in Ancient Rome, he also produced a number of poems such as the short verse above.

Mr T Lavelle of Preston requested it; he remembered learning it over sixty-five years ago when at school in Ireland.

THY SERVANT A DOG – HIS APOLOGIES
by Rudyard Kipling

Master, this is Thy Servant. He is rising eight weeks old.
He is mainly Head and Tummy. His legs are uncontrolled.
But Thou hast forgiven his ugliness, and settled him on Thy knee –
Art Thou content with Thy Servant? He is very comfy with Thee.

Master, behold a Sinner? He hath done grievous wrong.
He hath defiled Thy Premises through being kept in too long.
Wherefore his nose has been rubbed in the dirt, and his
self-respect has been bruisèd.
Master, pardon Thy Sinner, and see he is properly loosèd.

Master – again Thy Sinner! This that was once Thy Shoe,
He hath found and taken and carried aside, as fitting matter to chew.
Now there is neither blacking nor tongue, and the Housemaid
has us in tow.
Master, remember Thy Servant is young, and tell her to let him go!

Master, extol Thy Servant! He hath met a most Worthy Foe!
There has been fighting all over the Shop – and into the Shop also!
Till cruel umbrellas parted the strife (or I might have been
choking him yet).
But Thy Servant has had the Time of his Life – and now shall
we call on the vet?

Master, behold Thy Servant! Strange children came to play,
And because they fought to caress him, Thy Servant wentedst away.
But now that the Little Beasts have gone, he has returned to see
(Brushed – with his Sunday collar on –) what they left over
from tea.

Master, pity Thy Servant! He is deaf and three parts blind,
He cannot catch Thy Commandments. He cannot read Thy Mind.
Oh, leave him not in his loneliness; nor make him that
kitten's scorn.
He has had none other God than Thee since the year that he
was born!

Lord, look down on Thy Servant! Bad things have come to pass,
There is no heat in the midday sun nor health in the wayside grass.
His bones are full of an old disease – his torments run and increase.
Lord, make haste with Thy Lightnings and grant him a
quick release!

This poem comes from Kipling's story Thy Servant A Dog, *published in 1930. Margaret Taylor of Hawkwell requested it.*

SHEEP AND LAMBS
by Katharine Tynan Hinkson

All in the April evening,
April airs were abroad;
The sheep with their little lambs
Pass'd me by on the road.

The sheep with their little lambs
Pass'd me by on the road;
All in an April evening
I thought on the Lamb of God.

The lambs were weary, and crying
With a weak human cry,
I thought on the Lamb of God
Going meekly to die.

Up in the blue, blue mountains,
Dewy pastures are sweet:
Rest for the little bodies,
Rest for the little feet.

But for the Lamb of God
Up on the hill-top green,
Only a cross of shame
Two stark crosses between.

All in the April evening,
April airs were abroad;
I saw the sheep with their lambs,
And thought on the Lamb of God.

Katharine Tynan Hinkson (1861–1931)
Katharine Tynan Hinkson was a prolific Irish writer and poet who is said to have written over one hundred novels. The above verse held beautiful memories for L Hardiman-Hunt of Stansted, Essex, who recalled it being read or sung to him by a teacher at infant school.

DARWIN'S MISTAKE
Anonymous

Three monkeys sat in a coconut tree
Discussing things as they're said to be.
Said one to the other, 'Now listen you two,
There's a certain rumor that cannot be true.

That man descends from our noble race—
The very idea! It's a dire disgrace!
No monkey ever deserted his wife,
Starved her baby or ruined her life.

And you've never known a mother monk
To leave her babies with others to bunk,
And pass them around from one to another,
Till they scarcely know who is their mother.

And another thing, you'll never see
A monk build a fence around a coconut tree,
And let the coconuts go to waste,
Forbidding all other monks a taste.

Why if I put a fence around this tree,
Starvation would force you to steal from me.
Here's another thing a monk won't do,
Go out at night and get on a stew;

Or use a gun or club or knife
To take some other monkey's life.
Yes, man descended, the ornery cuss,
But brother, he didn't descend from us!'

Also known under the title 'The Monkey's Disgrace', this witty poem has even been set to music, but nobody knows who wrote it. Anthony Devlin of Birmingham, who remembers his mother reciting it, requested the verse.

GRASSHOPPER GREEN
Traditional

Grasshopper Green is a comical chap;
He lives on the best of fare.
Bright little trousers, jacket and cap,
These are his summer wear.
Out in the meadow he loves to go,
Playing away in the sun;
It's hopperty, skipperty, high and low—
Summer's the time for fun.

Grasshopper Green has a dozen wee boys,
And soon as their legs grow strong
Each of them joins in his frolicsome joys,
Singing his merry song.
Under the hedge in a happy row
Soon as the day has begun
It's hopperty, skipperty, high and low—
Summer's the time for fun.

Grasshopper Green has a quaint little house.
It's under the hedge so gay.
Grandmother Spider, as still as a mouse,
Watches him over the way.
Gladly he's calling the children, I know,
Out in the beautiful sun;
It's hopperty, skipperty, high and low—
Summer's the time for fun.

This traditional rhyme brought back memories for Linda Woolgar, who e-mailed us in search of it: 'In my first year at Primary school, I was asked to take part in a school Christmas show where I had to recite a poem that I could do actions to. My mum practised with me every day helping me to remember the lines of the poem and add the funniest of actions you can imagine – a five-year-old jumping and hoping all over the place.'

THE ANT AND THE CRICKET
Anonymous

A silly young cricket, accustomed to sing
Through the warm, sunny months of gay summer
and spring,
Began to complain, when he found that at home
His cupboard was empty and winter was come.
Not a crumb to be found
On the snow-covered ground;
Not a flower could he see,
Not a leaf on a tree.
'Oh, what will become,' says the cricket, 'of me?'

At last by starvation and famine made bold,
All dripping with wet and all trembling with cold,
Away he set off to a miserly ant
To see if, to keep him alive, he would grant
Him shelter from rain.
A mouthful of grain
He wished only to borrow,
He'd repay it to-morrow;
If not, he must die of starvation and sorrow.

Says the ant to the cricket: 'I'm your servant and friend,
But we ants never borrow, we ants never lend.
Pray tell me, dear sir, did you lay nothing by
When the weather was warm?' Said the cricket, 'Not I.
My heart was so light
That I sang day and night,
For all nature looked gay.'
'You sang, sir, you say?
Go then,' said the ant, 'and sing winter away.'

Thus ending, he hastily lifted the wicket
And out of the door turned the poor little cricket.
Though this is a fable, the moral is good—
If you live without work, you must live without food.

This poem is an anonymous adaptation of one of Aesop's Fables *and was on the required reading list, years ago, of many schools that wished to inspire a responsible work ethic among their students. Mrs V Jenkins of Maesteg, Mid-Glamorgan, requested it, with fond memories of such a school.*

THE RABBIT
by Georgia Roberts Durston

There once was a rabbit, who had the bad habit
Of twitching the end of his nose.
His sisters and brothers, and various others, said
'Look at the way he goes!'

But one little bunny said, 'Isn't it funny!'
And practised it down in the dell.
Said the others, 'If he can, I'm positive we can'
And did it remarkably well.

Now, all the world over, where rabbits eat clover
And burrow and scratch with their toes,
You'll find every rabbit has got the bad habit
Of twitching the end of his nose.

Georgia Roberts Durston (dates unknown)
Georgia Roberts Durston was an American children's writer and poet who wrote in the early 1900s.

This request came from Ann Miles of Gloucester with a nice history accompanying it: 'In the 1940s, my grandfather used to keep rabbits, partly for showing, but mainly for the table to eke out the meat ration. One week, he showed me a poem in Fur and Feather *magazine and taught it to me to recite at all the church concerts. It was about a rabbit that developed a habit of twitching the end of his nose. Can you help, as I should like to pass it on to my grandchildren?'*

6.

Humanity

SONNET 106
by William Shakespeare

When in the chronicle of wasted time
I see descriptions of the fairest wights,
And beauty making beautiful old rhyme
In praise of ladies dead and lovely knights,
Then, in the blazon of sweet beauty's best,
Of hand, of foot, of lip, of eye, of brow,
I see their antique pen would have express'd
Even such a beauty as you master now.
So all their praises are but prophecies
Of this our time, all you prefiguring;
And, for they look'd but with divining eyes,
They had not skill enough your worth to sing:
For we, which now behold these present days,
Had eyes to wonder, but lack tongues to praise.

In this verse, Shakespeare praises the skills of past poets in describing the most worthy and fairest people of their time ('wights' is an old word, archaic even in Shakespeare's time, for men and women) and laments the inability of poets of his time, who 'have eyes to wonder, but lack tongues to praise'. We went in search of this for Dorothy Black, who emailed to ask: 'Can you tell me where the phrase "chronicle of wasted time" comes from? I have a dim memory of seeing it in a poem or perhaps a Shakespeare play. I know it's been borrowed by several modern authors, but I'm sure it's much older.'

WANDERTHIRST
by Gerald Gould

Beyond the East the sunrise, beyond the West the sea,
And East and West, the Wanderthirst that will not let me be.
It works in me like madness dear, to be say goodbye,
For the seas call and the stars call, and, oh, the call of the sky.

I know not where the white road runs, nor what the blue hills are,
But I can have the sun for a friend, and for my guide a star.
And there's no end to voyaging, when once the call is heard;
For the river calls, the road calls, and oh! the call of the bird.

And if you should ask me, I could not tell you why;
But you can blame it on the white road, the blue hills, and the sky.
Beyond the long horizon lies, and there by night and day
The old ships draw to home again, and the young ships sail away.

Gerald Gould (1885–1936)
*Gerald Gould was primarily a journalist and reviewer who also wrote a good
deal of poetry for newspapers and magazines. This is perhaps his best-known
work, extolling the joy of travel and adventure.*

*It was requested by A McDonough of Elgin, Morayshire, who said that he
remembered the title and the first verse, but no more.*

BETWEEN MIDNIGHT AND MORNING
by Sir Owen Seaman

You that have faith to look with fearless eyes
Beyond the tragedy of a world at strife,
And trust that out of night and death shall rise
The dawn of ampler life;

Rejoice, whatever anguish rend your heart,
That God has given you, for a priceless dower,
To live in these great times and have your part
In Freedom's crowning hour.

That you may tell your sons who see the light
High in the heaven their heritage to take:
'I saw the powers of darkness put to flight!
I saw the morning break!'

Sir Owen Seaman (1861–1936)
Schoolmaster, professor of literature, and barrister, Sir Owen Seaman also
contributed light verse to Punch *magazine of which he later became editor.*
One of his assistants at Punch *was A A Milne, author of the Winnie-the-Pooh*
stories, and it is said that Seaman's sour demeanour inspired the character of
Eeyore. The above verse is one of his more serious efforts and was requested
by Greg Webb of Devizes, Wiltshire.

L'ENVOI
by Rudyard Kipling

When Earth's last picture is painted, and the tubes are
twisted and dried,
When the oldest colours have faded, and the youngest
critic has died,
We shall rest, and, faith, we shall need it – lie down for an
aeon or two,
Till the Master of All Good Workmen shall set us to
work anew!

And those who were good shall be happy: they shall sit
in a golden chair;
They shall splash at a ten-league canvas with brushes of
comet's hair;
They shall find real saints to draw from – Magdalene,
Peter, and Paul;
They shall work for an age at a sitting and never be
tired at all!

And only the Master shall praise us, and only the Master
shall blame;
And no one shall work for money, and no one shall
work for fame;
But each for the joy of the working, and each, in his
separate star,
Shall draw the Thing as he sees It for the God of Things
as They Are!

---

*This is a typically effective poem by Kipling, combining spirituality with the
harshness of the real world. George Howell of Doncaster requested this.*

ON THE HURRY OF THIS TIME
by Austin Dobson

With slower pen men used to write,
Of old, when 'letters' were 'polite';
In Anna's or in George's days,
They could afford to turn a phrase,
Or trim a struggling theme aright.

They knew not steam; electric light
Not yet had dazed their calmer sight; –
They meted out both blame and praise
With slower pen.

Too swiftly now the hours take flight!
What's read at morn is dead at night:
Scant space have we for Art's delays,
Whose breathless thought so briefly stays,
We may not work – ah! would we might! –
With slower pen.

This is a typically witty and perceptive piece by Austin Dobson, perhaps even more relevant in these days of emails and text messaging than when he wrote it. Brian Hillman of North London requested the poem.

SONNET 64
by William Shakespeare

When I have seen by Time's fell hand defaced
The rich proud cost of outworn buried age;
When sometime lofty towers I see down-razed
And brass eternal slave to mortal rage;
When I have seen the hungry ocean gain
Advantage on the kingdom of the shore,
And the firm soil win of the watery main,
Increasing store with loss and loss with store;
When I have seen such interchange of state,
Or state itself confounded to decay;
Ruin hath taught me thus to ruminate,
That Time will come and take my love away.
This thought is as a death, which cannot choose
But weep to have that which it fears to lose.

This is another of Shakespeare's sonnets with an often-quoted opening line.
Maureen Fox requested it, and described it as 'a poem that made a huge
impression on me towards the end of my schooldays'.

THE COMMON STREET
by Helen Gray Cone

The common street climbed up against the sky,
Gray meeting gray; and wearily to and fro
I saw the patient, common people go,
Each with his sordid burden trudging by.
And the rain dropped; there was not any sigh
Or stir of a live wind; dull, dull and slow
All motion; as a tale told long ago
The faded world; and creeping night drew nigh.

Then burst the sunset, flooding far and fleet,
Leavening the whole of life with magic leaven.
Suddenly down the long wet glistening hill
Pure splendor poured – and lo! the common street
A golden highway into golden heaven,
With the dark shapes of men ascending still.

Helen Gray Cone (1859–1934)
Helen Gray Cone was an American poet and Professor of English Literature in New York. We found this poem for eighty-five-year-old C R Gray of Macclesfield, who wrote: 'Neither love nor money has enabled me to find "The Common Street" by Helen Gray Cone, which was taught to me at school in the early 1930s. I have been trying for some time to get all the words and it would make my day if you could find it.'

THE ANVIL
by John Clifford

I paused last eve beside the blacksmith's door,
And heard the anvil ring, the vespers chime,
And looking in I saw upon the floor
Old hammers, worn with beating years of time.

'How many anvils have you had?' said I,
'To wear and batter all those hammers so?'
'Just one,' he answered. Then with twinkling eye:
'The anvil wears the hammers out, you know.'

And so, I thought, the anvil of God's Word
For ages skeptics' blows have beat upon,
But though the noise of falling blows was heard
The anvil is unchanged; the hammer's gone.

John Clifford (1836–1923)
John Clifford was a Baptist minister and social reformer who spent much of his life campaigning against what he saw as injustices, including a campaign against the Boer War and a long battle against the Education Acts of 1870 and 1902. The above poem, about the Anvil of God's word, was requested by RL Johnstone of Bricham, Cumbria, who told us that his godfather used to recite it to him seventy-five years ago.

THE DAY IS DONE
by Henry Wadsworth Longfellow

The day is done, and the darkness
Falls from the wings of Night,
As a feather is wafted downward
From an eagle in his flight.

I see the lights of the village
Gleam through the rain and the mist,
And a feeling of sadness comes o'er me
That my soul cannot resist:

A feeling of sadness and longing,
That is not akin to pain,
And resembles sorrow only
As the mist resembles the rain.

Come, read to me some poem,
Some simple and heartfelt lay,
That shall soothe this restless feeling,
And banish the thoughts of day.

Not from the grand old masters,
Not from the bards sublime,
Whose distant footsteps echo
Through the corridors of Time.

For, like strains of martial music,
Their mighty thoughts suggest
Life's endless toil and endeavour;
And tonight I long for rest.

Read from some humbler poet,
Whose songs gushed from his heart,
As showers from the clouds of summer,
Or tears from the eyelids start;

Who, through long days of labor,
And nights devoid of ease,
Still heard in his soul the music
Of wonderful melodies.

Such songs have power to quiet
The restless pulse of care,
And come like the benediction
That follows after prayer.

Then read from the treasured volume
The poem of thy choice,
And lend to the rhyme of the poet
The beauty of thy voice.

And the night shall be filled with music,
And the cares, that infest the day,
Shall fold their tents, like the Arabs,
And as silently steal away.

Charles Williamson requested this in an e-mail: 'For some few years now I have been bugged by a verse and I would dearly love to find the rest of it and the title and writer'. He quoted the final verse and we found the rest for him.

THE VILLAGE SCHOOLMASTER
by Oliver Goldsmith

Beside yon straggling fence that skirts the way
With blossom'd furze unprofitably gay,
There, in his mansion, skill'd to rule,
The village master taught his little school;
A man severe he was, and stern to view,
I knew him well, and every truant knew;
Well had the boding tremblers learn'd to trace
The day's disasters in his morning face;
Full well they laugh'd with counterfeited glee,
At all his jokes, for many a joke had he:
Full well the busy whisper, circling round,
Convey'd the dismal tidings when he frown'd:
Yet he was kind; or if severe in aught,
The love he bore to learning was in fault.
The village all declar'd how much he knew;
'Twas certain he could write, and cipher too:
Lands he could measure, terms and tides presage,
And e'en the story ran that he could gauge.
In arguing too, the parson own'd his skill,
For e'en though vanquish'd he could argue still;
While words of learned length and thund'ring sound
Amazed the gazing rustics rang'd around;
And still they gaz'd and still the wonder grew,
That one small head could carry all he knew.
But past is all his fame. The very spot
Where many a time he triumph'd is forgot.

Oliver Goldsmith (1728–74)
Best known for his play She Stoops To Conquer *and the novel* The Vicar of Wakefield, *Oliver Goldsmith also composed some fine poetry. The above verse was requested in an e-mail by Derrick Lamb, who remembered the lines about 'laughing with counterfeiting glee, at all his jokes, for many a joke had he', but said that was unfortunately all he knew.*

FROLIC
by George William Russell

The children were shouting together
And racing along the sands,
A glimmer of dancing shadows,
A dovelike flutter of hands.

The stars were shouting in heaven,
The sun was chasing the moon:
The game was the same as the children's,
They danced to the self-same tune.

The whole of the world was merry,
One joy from the vale to the height,
Where the blue woods of twilight encircled
The lovely lawns of the light.

George William Russell (1867–1935)
Poet, painter, and Irish nationalist, George William Russell was one of the
leading figures in Irish literature in the early years of the twentieth century.
Eighty-five-year-old Lydia Lingen-Hodges of Broomyard, Herefordshire,
who remembered it being read to her by her mother many years ago,
requested this verse.

THE LADY OF LAMBS
by Alice Meynell

She walks – the lady of my delight –
A shepherdess of sheep.
Her flocks are thoughts. She keeps them white;
She guards them from the steep.
She feeds them on the fragrant height,
And folds them in for sleep.

She roams maternal hills and bright,
Dark valleys safe and deep.
Her dreams are innocent at night;
The chastest stars may peep.
She walks – the lady of my delight –
A shepherdess of sleep.

She holds her little thoughts in sight,
Though gay they run and leap.
She is so circumspect and right;
She has her soul to keep.
She walks – the lady of my delight –
A shepherdess of sheep.

Alice Meynell (1847–1922)
Alice Meynell was a remarkable woman. Writer, editor, magazine publisher,
critic, and suffragette, she was a deeply religious woman whose beliefs come
through strongly in her work.

ON FIRST LOOKING INTO
CHAPMAN'S HOMER
by John Keats

Much have I travell'd in the realms of gold,
And many goodly states and kingdoms seen;
Round many western islands have I been
Which bards in fealty to Apollo hold.
Oft of one wide expanse had I been told
That deep-brow'd Homer ruled as his demesne:
Yet did I never breathe its pure serene
Till I heard Chapman speak out loud and bold:
Then felt I like some watcher of the skies
When a new planet swims into his ken;
Or like stout Cortez, when with eagle eyes
He stared at the Pacific – and all his men
Look'd at each other with a wild surmise –
Silent, upon a peak in Darien.

*This is a wonderfully evocative sonnet by Keats, expressing the joy of first
reading a translation of the works of Homer. The poet likens the discovery of
a great work of literature to the first sight of a new continent.*

*It was requested by Michael Fletcher of Walsall, who wrote: 'When
browsing through travel brochures and planning holidays, my late father used
often to say the lines "Much have I travelled in the realms of gold, and many
goodly states and kingdoms seen". I'm sure he knew where they came from,
but I never asked him.'*

LOSS AND GAIN
by Henry Wadsworth Longfellow

When I compare
What I have lost with what I have gained,
What I have missed with what attained,
Little room do I find for pride.

I am aware
How many days have been idly spent;
How like an arrow the good intent
Has fallen short or been turned aside.

But who shall dare
To measure loss and gain in this wise?
Defeat may be victory in disguise;
The lowest ebb is the turn of the tide.

Longfellow is best known for such epics as 'Hiawatha', but he is also the author of some thoughtful short verses such as the above, which was requested by Mr A Wilkinson of Durham.

SOLITUDE
by Alexander Pope

Happy the man, whose wish and care
A few paternal acres bound,
Content to breathe his native air
In his own ground.

Whose herds with milk, whose fields with bread,
Whose flocks supply him with attire;
Whose trees in summer yield him shade,
In winter, fire.

Blest, who can unconcern'dly find
Hours, days, and years slide soft away
In health of body, peace of mind,
Quiet by day,

Sound sleep by night; study and ease
Together mixed, sweet recreation,
And innocence, which most does please
With meditation.

Thus let me live, unseen, unknown;
Thus unlamented let me die;
Steal from the world, and not a stone
Tell where I lie.

Alexander Pope (1688–1733)
A recent edition of the Oxford Dictionary of Quotations *included more quotations from Alexander Pope than any other writer except Shakespeare and Tennyson. This poem beautifully captures the tranquility of solitude, with the calmness emphasised by the short final lines of each verse.*

AFTER ALL
by Henry Lawson

The brooding ghosts of Australian night have gone from
the bush and town;
My spirit revives in the morning breeze, though it died when
the sun went down;
The river is high and the stream is strong, and the grass is
green and tall,
And I fain would think that this world of ours is a
good world after all.

The light of passion in dreamy eyes, and a page of
truth well read,
The glorious thrill in a heart grown cold of the spirit
I thought was dead,
A song that goes to a comrade's heart, and a tear of pride
let fall
And my soul is strong! and the world to me is a
grand world after all!

Let our enemies go by their old dull tracks, and theirs be
the fault or shame
(The man is bitter against the world who has only
himself to blame);
Let the darkest side of the past be dark, and only
the good recall;
For I must believe that the world, my dear, is a
kind world after all.

It well may be that I saw too plain, and it may be
I was blind;
But I'll keep my face to the dawning light, though the devil
may stand behind!
Though the devil may stand behind my back, I'll not see
his shadow fall,
But read the signs in the morning stars of a
good world after all.

Rest, for your eyes are weary, girl – you have driven
the worst away –
The ghost of the man that I might have been is gone
from my heart to-day;
We'll live for life and the best it brings till our twilight
shadows fall;
My heart grows brave, and the world, my girl, is a
good world after all.

Henry Lawson (1867–1922)
*Henry Lawson was an Australian poet who became a celebrity as much for
his drunken exploits as his writings. Nevertheless, on his death he was given a
state funeral, and his picture appeared in 1966 on the Australian ten-dollar
note. This was been requested by Mrs JC Muncaster of Ilkley, West Yorks,
who heard it on the BBC radio programme 'Home And Away'.*

NON NOBIS DOMINE!
by Rudyard Kipling

Non nobis Domine!—
Not unto us, O Lord!
The Praise or Glory be
Of any deed or word;
For in Thy Judgment lies
To crown or bring to nought
All knowledge or device
That Man has reached or wrought.

And we confess our blame—
How all too high we hold
That noise which men call Fame,
That dross which men call Gold.
For these we undergo
Our hot and godless days,
But in our hearts we know
Not unto us the Praise.

O Power by Whom we live—
Creator, Judge, and Friend,
Upholdingly forgive
Nor fail us at the end:
But grant us well to see
In all our piteous ways—
Non nobis Domine!—
Not unto us the Praise!

This poem was written by Rudyard Kipling in 1934 for 'The Pageant of Parliament' and was requested by E Shields of Stanley, Co Durham, who remembered singing it at the London Olympic Games in 1948 and wanted to see it again 'even though some of the sentiments may seem outdated'.

7.

Death

and Disaster

THE PRIVATE OF THE BUFFS
by Sir Francis Hastings Charles Doyle

Last night, among his fellow roughs,
    He jested, quaff'd and swore,
A drunken private of the Buffs,
    Who never look'd before.
Today, beneath the foeman's frown
    He stands in Elgin's place,
Ambassador from Britain's Crown
    And type of all her race.

Poor, reckless, rude, low-born, untaught,
    Bewilder'd and alone.
A heart, with English instinct fraught,
    He yet can call his own.
Aye, tear his body limb from limb,
    Bring cord, or axe, or flame;
He only knows that not through him
    Shall England come to shame.

Far Kentish hop fields round him seem'd
    Like dreams, to come and go;
Bright leagues of cherry blossom gleam'd,
    One sheet of living snow;
The smoke above his father's door
    In grey soft eddyings hung.
Must he then watch it rise no more,
    Doom'd by himself so young?

Yes, honour calls!—with strength like steel
He puts the vision by.
Let dusky Indians whine and kneel;
An English lad must die.
And thus, with eyes that would not shrink,
With knee to man unbent,
Unfaltering on its dreadful brink
To his red grave he went.

Vain, mightiest fleets of iron fram'd;
Vain, those all-shattering guns;
Unless proud England keep, untam'd
The strong heart of her sons.
So, let his name through England ring—
A man of mean estate,
Who died, as firm as Sparta's king
Because his soul was great.

Sir Francis Hastings Charles Doyle (1810–88)
*Sir Francis Hastings Charles Doyle was a poet and civil servant, serving in
the customs department. He was also Professor of Poetry at Oxford, and best
man at William Gladstone's wedding.*

*The poem above was requested by Roy Armstrong of Farnham, Surrey,
who tells us his father taught it to him around 1930. It was written in memory
of English Private John Moyse, who was killed by the Chinese in 1860 during
the Second Opium War.*

OH! SNATCHED AWAY IN BEAUTY'S BLOOM
by George Gordon, Lord Byron

Oh! snatched away in beauty's bloom,
On thee shall press no ponderous tomb;
But on thy turf shall roses rear
Their leaves, the earliest of the year;
And the wild cypress wave in tender gloom:

And oft by yon blue gushing stream
Shall sorrow lean her drooping head,
And feed deep thought with many a dream,
And lingering pause and lightly tread;
Fond wretch! as if her step disturbed the dead!

Away! ye know that tears are vain,
That death nor heeds nor hears distress:
Will this unteach us to complain?
Or make one mourner weep the less?
And thou – who tell'st me to forget,
Thy looks are wan, thine eyes are wet.

George Gordon, Lord Byron (1788–1824)
George Gordon Byron, the sixth Baron Byron, inherited the title and its associated estates from his uncle at the age of ten. Originally refused burial in Westminster Abbey owing to his notoriety, he was finally granted a plaque in Poets' Corner there in 1969.

Paul Robinson of Slough requested the poem after hearing it read at a funeral of a young friend many years ago.

REQUIESCAT
by Matthew Arnold

Strew on her roses, roses,
And never a spray of yew.
In quiet she reposes:
Ah! would that I did too.

Her mirth the world required:
She bathed it in smiles of glee.
But her heart was tired, tired,
And now they let her be.

Her life was turning, turning,
In mazes of heat and sound.
But for peace her soul was yearning,
And now peace laps her round.

Her cabin'd, ample Spirit,
It flutter'd and fail'd for breath.
To-night it doth inherit
The vasty hall of Death.

Matthew Arnold (1822–88)
*Matthew Arnold was a poet, critic, and inspector of schools; he was also the
son of the famous Rugby School headmaster Thomas Arnold. This is one of his
lesser-known works, and was requested by Margaret Allen from Winchester
who remembered hearing it read at her mother's funeral, which was held in a
beautiful rose-filled graveyard. As she said, however, 'it was the line about
"bathing the world in smiles of glee" that seemed so apt.'*

THE MISTLETOE BOUGH
by **Thomas Haynes Bayly**

The mistletoe hung in the castle hall,
The holly branch shone on the old oak wall;
And the baron's retainers were blithe and gay,
And keeping their Christmas holiday.
The baron beheld with a father's pride
His beautiful child, young Lovell's bride;
While she with her bright eyes seemed to be
The star of the goodly company.

'I'm weary of dancing now,' she cried;
'Here, tarry a moment? I'll hide? I'll hide!
And, Lovell, be sure thou'rt first to trace
The clew to my secret lurking place.'
Away she ran – and her friends began
Each tower to search, and each nook to scan;
And young Lovell cried, 'O, where dost thou hide?
I'm lonesome without thee, my own dear bride.'

They sought her that night! and they sought her next day!
And they sought her in vain while a week passed away!
In the highest, the lowest, the loneliest spot,
Young Lovell sought wildly – but found her not.
And years flew by, and their grief at last
Was told as a sorrowful tale long past;
And when Lovell appeared the children cried,
'See! the old man weeps for his fairy bride.'

At length an oak chest, that had long lain hid,
Was found in the castle – they raised the lid,
And a skeleton form lay moldering there
In the bridal wreath of that lady fair!
O, sad was her fate! – in sportive jest
She hid from her lord in the old oak chest.
It closed with a spring! – and, dreadful doom,
The bride lay clasp'd in her living tomb!

Thomas Haynes Bayly (1797–1839)
Thomas Haynes Bayly was best known as a songwriter, writing hundreds of lyrics as well as novels and poetry. The above verse is a splendid nineteenth-century horror story. Mrs M Whitaker of Blackburn told us that her mother used to recite it to her when she was young: 'I always thought it was very sad,' she commented.

REQUIEM
by Robert Louis Stevenson

Under the wide and starry sky,
Dig the grave and let me lie.
Glad did I live and gladly die,
And I laid me down with a will.

This be the verse you grave for me:
Here he lies where he long'd to be;
Home is the sailor, home from sea,
And the hunter home from the hill.

This short poem can be seen inscribed on Robert Louis Stevenson's gravestone in Samoa. It was requested by Mrs R Sparkes from Chichester, who told us that her sister's class at school used to recite it, 'always in a mournful voice', while air-raid alerts were going on during the Second World War.

THE DYING FIREMAN
by Walt Whitman

I am the mashed fireman with breast-bone broken,
Tumbling walls buried me in their debris,
Heat and smoke I inspired, I heard the yelling shouts of
my comrades,
I heard the distant click of their picks and shovels;
They have cleared the beams away, they tenderly lift
me forth.

I lie in the night air in my red shirt, the pervading hush is
for my sake,
Painless after all I lie exhausted but not so unhappy,
White and beautiful are the faces around me, the heads are
bared of their firecaps,
The kneeling crowd fades with the light of the torches.

Walt Whitman (1819–92)
*Walt Whitman was an American poet, whose writing captured, perhaps
better than anyone else, the spirit of the early United States.*
   *Vera Ball from Waddington, Lincs, asked for this grim but uplifting verse:
'I should be glad if you could trace a poem from my schooldays. It's about
a dying fireman who "lies in the night air in his red shirt, his breast bone
broken".' This is only a small extract of the Heroes sections of the much-longer
'Song of Myself'.*

TO THE MOTHER
by Katharine Tynan Hinkson

I heard them talking and praising the grey French country,
    Dotted with red roofs high and steep,
With just one grey stone church-tower keeping sentry
    Over the quiet dead asleep;
Grey skies and greyer dunes, as grey as duty,
    Grey sands where grey gulls flew;
And I said in my passionate heart, they know not beauty,
    Beloved, who know not you.

I heard them praise the gold of the stormy sunset
    And the pale moon's path on the sea;
I thought of your clouds with their wild magnificent onset,
    Your eagles screaming free.
I thought of your mild, kind mountains, angel-bosomed,
    Quiet in dusk and dew.
What flower of beauty that ever in Paradise blossomed,
    Love, was denied to you?

I thought of the pale green dawns, and gold days' closes.
    Dear, I shall not forget
Nights when your skies were full of the flying roses,
    Millions and millions yet.
All your still lakes and your rivers broad and gracious,
    Dear mountain glens I knew;
When the trump of judgment sounds and the world's in ashes
    I shall remember you.

Remember! foretaste of Heaven you are, O Mother!
By bog-lands, brown and bare,
Where every little pool is the blue sky's brother,
Your wild larks spring in the air.
Land of my heart! smiling I heard their praises,
Smiling and sighing too.
I would give this grey French land for a handful of daisies
Plucked from the breast of you.

Mrs J Campbell from Blackpool asked for this poem 'on behalf of a very dear friend who is in her ninetieth year'. As she says, the 'Mother' referred to in its title is the writer's mother country of Ireland.

DO NOT STAND AT MY GRAVE AND WEEP
by Mary Elizabeth Frye

Do not stand at my grave and weep;
I am not there. I do not sleep.
I am a thousand winds that blow.
I am the diamond glints on snow.
I am the sunlight on ripened grain.
I am the gentle autumn rain.
When you awaken in the morning's hush
I am the swift uplifting rush
Of quiet birds in circled flight.
I am the soft stars that shine at night.
Do not stand at my grave and cry;
I am not there. I did not die.

Mary Elizabeth Frye (1905–2004)
This is an extraordinary poem with a history to match. There is some doubt about its authorship – there has even been a suggestion that it is a Navajo burial verse – but the general consensus is that it was written by an American, Mary, who was deeply touched by the plight of a German–Jewish girl she met in 1932. The girl was upset at not being able to weep by the grave of her mother who had just died in Germany. Mary Frye, who had never written a poem before and never published or copyrighted this one, is said to have scribbled it on a brown paper bag. It has since established itself as one of the nation's favourites.

8.
Morality

THE HUMAN SEASONS
by John Keats

Four Seasons fill the measure of the year;
There are four seasons in the mind of man:
He has his lusty Spring, when fancy clear
Takes in all beauty with an easy span:
He has his summer, when luxuriously
Spring's honey'd cud of youthful thought he loves
To ruminate, and by such dreaming high
Is nearest unto heaven: quiet coves
His soul has in its Autumn, when his wings
He furleth close; contented so to look
On mists in idleness—to let fair things
Pass by unheeded as a threshold brook—
He has his Winter too of pale misfeature,
Or else he would forego his mortal nature.'

William Collins of Liverpool requested this, and said he was reminded of this verse when reading Shakespeare's 'Seven Ages Of Man' speech. While Shakespeare goes from babyhood through the delights of youth to the decrepitude of old age, Keats's version is more romantic and inward looking.

EASTER WEEK
by Charles Kingsley

See the land, her Easter keeping,
Rises as her Maker rose.
Seeds, so long in darkness sleeping,
Burst at last from winter snows.
Earth with heaven above rejoices;
Fields and gardens hail the spring;
Shaughs and woodlands ring with voices,
While the wild birds build and sing.

You, to whom your Maker granted
Powers to those sweet birds unknown,
Use the craft by God implanted;
Use the reason not your own.
Here, while heaven and earth rejoices,
Each his Easter tribute bring—
Work of fingers, chant of voices,
Like the birds who build and sing.

This verse was written to be sung at a Parish fair. Margaret Hales requested it in an email.

THE LOOM OF TIME
Anonymous

Man's life is laid in the loom of time
To a pattern he does not see,
While the weavers work and the shuttles fly
Till the dawn of eternity.

Some shuttles are filled with silver threads
And some with threads of gold,
While often but the darker hues
Are all that they may hold.

But the weaver watches with skilful eye
Each shuttle fly to and fro,
And sees the pattern so deftly wrought
As the loom moves sure and slow.

God surely planned the pattern:
Each thread, the dark and fair,
Is chosen by His master skill
And placed in the web with care.

He only knows its beauty,
And guides the shuttles which hold
The threads so unattractive,
As well as the threads of gold.

Not till each loom is silent,
And the shuttles cease to fly,
Shall God reveal the pattern
And explain the reason why

The dark threads were as needful
In the weaver's skilful hand
As the threads of gold and silver
For the pattern which He planned.

Catherine Lomas of Stevenage requested this poem and told us that it made a great impression on her many years ago. This verse has often appeared in collections of suitable poetry to be read at memorial services, but its author remains unknown.

TO-MORROW
by Benjamin Franklin

To-morrow you'll reform, you always cry;
In what far Country does this Morrow lie,
   That 'tis so mighty long e'er it arrive?
Beyond the Indies does this Morrow live?
'Tis so far-fetch'd, this Morrow, that I fear,
   'Twill be both very old, and very dear.
To-morrow I'll reform, the Fool does say:
Today itself's too late; — the Wise did yesterday.

Benjamin Franklin (1706–90)
This verse by the philosopher, statesman, and scientist Benjamin Franklin,
first appeared in 1737 in Poor Richard's Almanac. *Non Thomas of*
Pontypridd requested it.

WHAT IS GOOD?
by John Boyle O'Reilly

'What is the real good?'
I asked in musing mood.
'Order', said the law court;
'Knowledge', said the school;
'Truth', said the wise man;
'Pleasure', said the fool;
'Love', said the maiden;
'Beauty', said the page;
'Freedom', said the dreamer;
'Home', said the sage;
'Fame', said the soldier;
'Equity', the seer.
Spake my heart full sadly:
'The answer is not here.'

Then within my bosom
Softly this I heard:
'Each heart holds the secret:
"Kindness" is the word.'

John Boyle O'Reilly (1844–90)
*John Boyle O'Reilly was an Irish poet who was deported to Australia in his
youth for the crime of belonging to a republican organisation. He escaped to
the United States where he made his name as a writer in Boston. Margaret
Henderson of Liverpool, who remembered her parents having a copy of it
framed on the mantelpiece, requested the above verse.*

GIVE US MEN!
by Josiah Gilbert Holland

God give us men! a time like this demands
Strong minds, great hearts, true faith and ready hands;
Men whom the lust of office cannot kill;
Men whom the spoils of office cannot buy;
Men who possess opinions and a will;
Men who have honor; men who will not lie;
Men who can stand before a demagogue,
And damn his treacherous flatteries without winking!
Tall men, sun-crowned, who live above the fog
In public duty, and in private thinking;
For while the rabble, with its thumb-worn creeds,
Its large professions, and its little deeds,
Mingle in selfish strife, o! Freedom weeps,
Wrong rules the land, and waiting Justice sleeps.

Josiah Gilbert Holland (1819–81)
Josiah Gilbert Holland was an American poet and novelist. This was requested in an email from Robert Mitchell who said he was reminded of its sentiment – 'God give us men' – whenever we have an election or change of prime minister.

IF I KNEW
by Maud Wyman

If I knew a box where the smiles are kept,
No matter how large the key
Or strong the bolt, I would try so hard
'Twould open, I know, for me;
Then over the land and the sea broadcast,
I'd scatter the smiles to play,
That the children's faces might hold them fast
For many and many a day.

If I knew a box that was large enough
To hold all the frowns I meet,
I would like to gather them every one,
From the nursery, school, and street;
Then folding and holding, I'd pack them in,
And turning the monster key,
I'd hire a giant to drop the box
To the depths of the deep, deep sea.

Maud Wyman (dates unknown)
Maud Wyman was an American poet who wrote children's verse in the late nineteenth century. This was requested by Janet Lewis of Bedford, who remembered learning it when she was about eleven years old and lived in Newark, Notts.

THE NOBLE NATURE
by Ben Jonson

It is not growing like a tree
In bulk, doth make Man better be;
Or standing long an oak, three hundred year,
To fall a log at last, dry, bald, and sere:
A lily of a day
Is fairer far in May,
Although it fall and die that night –
It was the plant and flower of Light.
In small proportions we just beauties see;
And in short measures life may perfect be.

Ben Jonson (1572–1637)
Ben Jonson was a playwright and poet, and a contemporary of Shakespeare.
This verse comes from his 'Pindaric Ode on the Death of Sir H. Morison' and
was requested by Barbara Evans of Glamorgan.

9.

Humour

A REASONABLE AFFLICTION
by Matthew Prior

On his death-bed poor Lubin lies:
His spouse is in despair;
With frequent cries, and mutual sighs,
They both express their care.

'A different cause,' says Parson Sly,
'The same effect may give:
Poor Lubin fears that he may die;
His wife, that he may live.'

Matthew Prior (1664–1721)
Matthew Prior was a poet, satirist, diplomat, and gentleman of the King's
bedchamber to King William III. The wicked little verse above was requested
by John Morton in an email.

ALL SAINTS
by Edmund Yates

In a church which is furnished with mullion and gable,
With altar and reredos, with gargoyle and groin,
The penitents' dresses are sealskin and sable,
The odor of sanctity's eau-de-cologne.
But only could Lucifer, flying from Hades,
Gaze down on this crowd with its paniers and paints,
He would say, as he looked at the lords and the ladies,
'Oh, where is All Sinners' if this is All Saints'?'

Edmund Yates (1831–94)
Edmund Yates was a journalist, novelist, dramatist, and poet who also spent a period of his life working for the Post Office. Geoffrey Tate of Peterborough, who said he'd like to show it to his vicar, requested the above verse. 'He has a good sense of humour and I'm sure he'd enjoy it.'

THE CUDGEL'D HUSBAND
by Jonathan Swift

As Thomas was cudgel'd one day by his wife,
He took to his heels and fled for his life:
Tom's three dearest friends came by in the squabble,
And saved him at once from the shrew and the rabble;
Then ventured to give him some sober advice –
But Tom is a person of honour so nice,
Too wise to take counsel, too proud to take warning,
That he sent to all three a challenge next morning.
Three duels he fought, thrice ventured his life;
Went home, and was cudgeled again by his wife.

Jonathan Swift (1667–1745)
This is a delicious little piece of humour from the author of Gulliver's Travels.
*Although best known as the leading satirist of his time, Jonathan also wrote a
good deal of excellent poetry.*

A STRONG HAND
by Aaron Hill

Tenderhanded stroke a nettle,
And it stings you for your pains;
Grasp it like a lad of mettle,
And it soft as silk remains:
So it is with these fair creatures,
Use them kindly, they rebel;
But be rough as nutmeg graters,
And the rogues obey you well.

Aaron Hill (1685–1750)
Aaron Hill was an English dramatist. His little verse on how to handle
women was requested by John Williamson of Crewe, who assured us that
he was no misogynist, but said, 'I was amused by its comparison of women
with nettles.'

RIDING DOWN FROM BANGOR
by Louis Shreve Osborne

Riding down from Bangor, on an eastbound train,
After weeks of hunting, in the woods of Maine,
Quite extensive whiskers, beard, mustache as well,
Sat a student fellow, tall and slim and swell.

Empty seat behind him, no one at his side,
Into quiet village, eastern train did glide,
Enter aged couple, take the hindmost seat,
Enter village maiden, beautiful, petite.

Blushingly she faltered, 'Is this seat engaged?'
Sees the aged couple, properly enraged,
Student's quite ecstatic, sees her ticket through,
Thinks of the long tunnel, thinks of what he will do

Pleasantly they chatted, how the cinders fly
Til the student fellow, gets one in his eye
Maiden sympathetic, turns herself about
'May I if you please sir, try to get it out?'

Then the student fellow, feels a gentle touch
Hears a gentle murmur, 'Does it hurt you much?'
Whiz! Slap! Bang! Into the tunnel quite
Into glorious darkness, black as Egypt's night

Out into the daylight glides that eastern train
Student's hair is ruffled, just the merest grain
Maiden seen all blushes when then and there appeared
A tiny little earring, in that horrid student's beard.

Louis Shreve Osborne (1884–1912)

Louis Shreve Osborne was an American poet who is now almost solely remembered for this verse, which was turned into a song, and first published in the 1880s.

It was requested by Mrs R Markham from Merseyside, who admitted to having been confused by the idea of riding down to Bangor from the woods of Maine, until she realised that there is a Bangor in America as well as one in Wales.

THE DEVIL
by Robert Southey

From his brimstone bed at the break of day
A walking the Devil is gone
To visit his snug little farm, the earth
And see how his stock goes on.

Over the hill and over the dale,
And he went over the plain,
And backward and forward he switched his long tail
As a gentleman switches his cane.

And how then was the Devil dressed?
Oh! he was in his Sunday's best:
His jacket was red and his breeches were blue
And there was a hole where the tail came through.

Robert Southey (1774–1843)
Robert Southey was Poet Laureate and a prolific biographer, but his best-known work by far was The Story Of The Three Bears, *the original Goldilocks tale.*

THE WITCH
by Percy H Hott

I saw her plucking cowslips,
And marked her where she stood:
She never knew I watched her
While hiding in the wood.

Her skirt was brightest crimson,
And black her steeple hat,
Her broomstick lay beside her—
I'm positive of that.

Her chin was sharp and pointed,
Her eyes were—I don't know—
For, when she turned towards me—
I thought it best—to go!

Percy H Hott (dates unknown)
*Mrs P Stringer of Warrington requested this poem having remembered it as a
school poem from about sixty years ago: 'and it still haunts me'. This little
verse by Percy Hott has long been a favourite in Speech and Drama classes.*

BUILDERS' WARNING
Traditional

Sir Isaac Newton told us why,
An apple falls down from the sky,
And from this fact it's very plain,
All other objects do the same!

A brick, a bolt, a bar, a cup,
Invariably fall down, not up,
And every common working tool,
Is governed by this self-same rule!

So when you handle tools up there,
Let your watchword be 'Take Care'.
If, at work, you drop a spanner,
It travels in a downward manner!

At work, a fifth of accidents or more,
Illustrate old Newton's Law,
But one thing he forgot to add,
The damage won't be half as bad,
If you are wearing proper clothes,
Especially on your head and toes.

These hats and shoes are there to save
The wearer from an early grave.
So best foot forward and take care
About the kind of shoes you wear.

It's better to be sure than dead,
So get a hat and keep your head!
Don't think to go without is brave;
The effects of gravity can be grave!

Although this verse has frequently been spotted nailed to the wall or notice board on building sites, nobody knows where it originated. This was requested in an e-mail by Bob Yeames-Smith, who remembered it from a safety advert on television in the 1960s warning about the need to wear a safety helmet.

ERCEUS EXIT
by Austin Dobson

I intended an Ode,
And it turn'd to a Sonnet
It began à la mode,
I intended an Ode;
But Rose cross'd the road
In her latest new bonnet;
I intended an Ode;
And it turn'd to a Sonnet.

Neither an ode nor a sonnet, this is a triolet, with the same line repeated three times.

LITTLE ELFMAN
by John Kendrick Bangs

I met a little elfman once,
    Down where the lilies blow.
I asked him why he was so small,
    And why he didn't grow.

He slightly frowned, and with his eye
He looked me through and through—
    'I'm just as big for me,' said he,
    'As you are big for you!'

John Kendrick Bangs (1862–1922)
John Kendrick Bangs was an American author and satirist, whose fantasy books set in the afterlife gave rise to a genre of writing dubbed 'Bangsian fantasy'.

Wendy Mulkerrins, from Leigh in Surrey, asked to be reminded of it: 'My father used to say this ditty to me as a child, but as much as I loved to hear my dad recite it to me as though he was speaking to the elfman, I never ever committed it all to memory, and my father never wrote it down.'

THE STORY OF AUGUSTUS,
Who Would Not Have Any Soup
By Heinrich Hoffmann

Augustus was a chubby lad;
Fat ruddy cheeks Augustus had:
And everybody saw with joy
The plump and hearty, healthy boy.
He ate and drank as he was told,
And never let his soup get cold.
But one day, one cold winter's day,
He screamed out 'Take the soup away!
O take the nasty soup away!
I won't have any soup today.'

Next day, now look, the picture shows
How lank and lean Augustus grows!
Yet, though he feels so weak and ill,
The naughty fellow cries out still
'Not any soup for me, I say:
O take the nasty soup away!
I won't have any soup today.'

The third day comes: Oh what a sin!
To make himself so pale and thin.
Yet, when the soup is put on table,
He screams, as loud as he is able,
    'Not any soup for me, I say:
    O take the nasty soup away!
    I WON'T have any soup today.'

Look at him, now the fourth day's come!
He scarcely weighs a sugar-plum;
    He's like a little bit of thread,
And, on the fifth day, he was – dead!

Heinrich Hoffman (1809–94)
This poem comes from the nineteenth century children's book Struwwelpeter
*by Heinrich Hoffmann, a series of humorous poems about misbehaving
children. Appropriately enough, the author was a psychiatrist, and the first
person to identify hyperactivity in children.*

NOTHING TO SAY
by O Henry

'You can tell your paper,' the great man said,
'I refused an interview.
I have nothing to say on the question, sir;
Nothing to say to you.'

And then he talked till the sun went down
And the chickens went to roost;
And he seized the collar of the poor young man,
And never his hold he loosed.

And the sun went down and the moon came up,
And he talked till the dawn of day;
Though he said, 'On this subject mentioned by you
I have nothing whatever to say.'

And down the reporter dropped to sleep
And flat on the floor he lay;
And the last he heard was the great man's words,
I have nothing at all to say.'

O Henry (1862–1910)
O Henry was the pen name of the American writer William Sydney Porter,
who wrote around four hundred highly witty short stories.

REBECCA'S AFTER-THOUGHT
by Elizabeth Turner

Yesterday, Rebecca Mason,
In the parlour by herself,
Broke a handsome china basin,
Placed upon the mantel-shelf.

Quite alarmed, she thought of going
Very quietly away,
Not a single person knowing,
Of her being there that day.

But Rebecca recollected
She was taught deceit to shun;
And the moment she reflected,
Told her mother what was done;

Who commended her behaviour,
Loved her better, and forgave her.

Elizabeth Turner (dates unknown)
*Elizabeth Turner was an English children's poet who wrote in the first half of
the nineteenth century. The above verse is a typically moral poem from the
Victorian age, and was requested by M Cartlidge of Stoke-on-Trent.*

NO FAULT IN WOMEN
by Robert Herrick

No fault in women to refuse
The offer which they most would choose:
No fault in women to confess
How tedious they are in their dress:
No fault in women to lay on
The tincture of vermilion,
And there to give the cheek a dye
Of white, where Nature doth deny:
No fault in women to make show
Of largeness, when they're nothing so;
When, true it is, the outside swells
With inward buckram, little else:
No fault in women, though they be
But seldom from suspicion free:
No fault in womankind at all,
If they but slip, and never fall.

Robert Herrick (1591–1674)
The seventeenth-century poet Robert Herrick wrote a great deal of fine romantic verse, though he never married. Perhaps this poem explains why. It was requested by Robert James from Derby who said it was a poem 'which I've wanted for some time to read to my wife'.

10.
Children's Verse

AMY ELIZABETH ERMYNTRUDE ANNIE
by Queenie Scott-Hopper

Amy Elizabeth Ermyntrude Annie
Went to the country to visit her granny
Learnt to make butter and learnt to make cheese
Learnt to milk cows and take honey from bees
Learnt to spice roseleaves and learnt to cure ham
Learnt to make cider and blackcurrant jam.

When she came home she could not settle down
Said there was nothing to do in the town
Nothing to do and nothing to see
Life was all shopping and afternoon tea
Amy Elizabeth Ermyntrude Annie
Ran away back to the country and granny.

Queenie Scott-Hopper (dates unknown)
Queenie Scott-Hopper was a writer of children's stories and verse who flourished in the early twentieth century. This particular poem is one of her best known and was first requested by Adeline Reid from Keith in Banffshire, who recalled taking great joy from it during school elocution lessons, though all she could remember precisely were the first two lines.

SIX LITTLE MICE
by 'Mother Goose'

Six little mice sat down to spin;
Pussy passed by and she peeped in;
'What are you doing, my little men?'
'Weaving coats for gentlemen.'

'Shall I come in and cut off your threads?'
'No, no, Mistress Pussy, you'd bite off our heads.'
'Oh, no, I'll not; I'll help you to spin.'
'That may be so, but you can't come in!'

'Mother Goose' (dates unknown)
The origins of Mother Goose are hotly debated, with both Massachusetts and
France claiming to be the home of the original in the middle of the seventeenth
century. Charles Perrault published his Contes de ma Mère l'Oye *(Stories*
of My Mother Goose) in France in 1695, where many of the classic nursery
rhymes were printed for the first time.

Betty At The Party
Anonymous

'When I was at the party'
Said Betty, aged just four.
'A little girl fell off her chair,
Right down upon the floor;
And all the other little girls
Began to laugh, but me –
I didn't laugh a single bit,'
Said Betty seriously.

'Why not?' her mother asked her,
Full of delight to find
That Betty – bless her little heart –
Had been so sweetly kind.
'Why didn't you laugh, my darling?
Or don't you like to tell?'
'I didn't laugh,' said Betty,
' 'Cause it was me that fell.'

This is a popular rhyme, with a nice joke in its tail; Mrs P Beane of Norwich first requested it.

THERE WAS A LITTLE GIRL
by Henry Wadsworth Longfellow

There was a little girl,
Who had a little curl,
Right in the middle of her forehead.
And when she was good,
She was very, very good,
But when she was bad she was horrid.

There is some mystery about this verse, as Longfellow only admitted to having written 'that silly poem' when he was on his deathbed. Mr J Busby of Tonbridge, Kent told us that his mother used to recite it eighty years ago.

WEE WILLIE WINKIE
by William Miller

Wee Willie Winkie rins through the toun,
Up stairs and doon stairs in his nicht-goun,
Tirlin' at the window, cryin' at the lock,
'Are the weans in their bed, for it's noo ten o'clock?'

'Hey, Willie Winkie, are ye comin' ben?
The cat's singin' grey thrums to the sleepin' hen,
The dog's spelder'd on the floor, and disna gi'e a cheep,
But here's a waukrife laddie that winna fa' asleep!'

Onything but sleep, you rogue! Glow'ring like the mune,
Rattlin' in an airn jug wi' an airn spune,
Rumblin', tumblin' round about, crawin' like a cock,
Skirlin' like a kenna-what, wauk'nin' sleepin' folk.

'Hey, Willie Winkie – the wean's in a creel!
Wambling aff a bodie's knee like a verra eel,
Ruggin' at the cat's lug, and ravelin' a' her thrums
Hey, Willie Winkie – see, there he comes!'

Wearit is the mither that has a stoorie wean,
A wee stumple stoussie, that canna rin his lane,
That has a battle aye wi' sleep before he'll close an ee
But a kiss frae aff his rosy lips gies strength anew to me.

William Miller (1810–1872)

James Cornfield of Blantyre, Scotland, set us on the hunt for this verse, which, he said, he had learnt from his late parents who spoke in a broad Scots accent. 'The eldest in our family maintains that the poem was written by a man who lived in our village of Blantyre who was known as "The Poet Laureate of the Nursery".'

Mr Cornfield was right. William Miller wrote 'Wee Willie Winkie' in 1841, and he wrote it in Scots dialect. This is the original version. Those familiar with the better-known English translation will remember that children's bedtime was brought forward to eight o'clock south of the border.

THE UNSEEN PLAYMATE
by Robert Louis Stevenson

When children are playing alone on the green,
In comes the playmate that never was seen.
When children are happy and lonely and good,
The Friend of the Children comes out of the wood.

Nobody heard him and nobody saw,
His is a picture you never could draw,
But he's sure to be present, abroad or at home,
When children are happy and playing alone.

He lies in the laurels, he runs on the grass,
He sings when you tinkle the musical glass;
Whene'er you are happy and cannot tell why,
The Friend of the Children is sure to be by!

He loves to be little, he hates to be big,
'Tis he that inhabits the caves that you dig;
'Tis he when you play with your soldiers of tin
That sides with the Frenchman and never can win.

'Tis he, when at night you go off to your bed,
Bids you go to your sleep and not trouble your head;
For wherever they're lying, in cupboard or shelf,
'Tis he will take care of your playthings himself!

Mrs B Booth from Sheffield requested Stevenson's evocation of the imaginary playmate.

WHO KILLED COCK ROBIN
Anonymous

'Who killed Cock Robin?' 'I,' said the Sparrow,
'With my bow and arrow, I killed Cock Robin.'
'Who saw him die?' 'I,' said the Fly,
'With my little eye, I saw him die.'
'Who caught his blood?' 'I,' said the Fish,
'With my little dish, I caught his blood.'
'Who'll make the shroud?' 'I,' said the Beetle,
'With my thread and needle, I'll make the shroud.'
'Who'll dig his grave?' 'I,' said the Owl,
'With my pick and shovel, I'll dig his grave.'
'Who'll be the parson?' 'I,' said the Rook,
'With my little book, I'll be the parson.'
'Who'll be the clerk?' 'I,' said the Lark,
'If it's not in the dark, I'll be the clerk.'
'Who'll carry the link?' 'I,' said the Linnet,
'I'll fetch it in a minute, I'll carry the link.'
'Who'll be chief mourner?' 'I,' said the Dove,
'I mourn for my love, I'll be chief mourner.'
'Who'll carry the coffin?' 'I,' said the Kite,
'If it's not through the night, I'll carry the coffin.'
'Who'll bear the pall?' 'We,' said the Wren,
Both the cock and the hen, 'we'll bear the pall.'

'Who'll sing a psalm?' 'I,' said the Thrush,
As she sat on a bush, 'I'll sing a psalm.'
'Who'll toll the bell?' 'I,' said the bull,
'Because I can pull, I'll toll the bell.'
All the birds of the air fell a-sighing and a-sobbing,
When they heard the bell toll for poor Cock Robin.

This is a nursery rhyme with a long history, though nobody knows where it started. Some say – with no evidence whatsoever – that it relates to Robin Hood, others that it refers to prime minister Robert Walpole. It was first published in 1744 in Tommy Thumb's Song Book, *the first collection of nursery rhymes published in England.*

LET DOGS DELIGHT
by Isaac Watts

Let dogs delight to bark and bite,
For God hath made them so;
Let bears and lions growl and fight,
For 'tis their nature too.
But, children, you should never let
Such angry passions rise;
Your little hands were never made
To tear each other's eyes.

Isaac Watts (1674–1748)
Isaac Watts was a prolific hymn-writer in the late seventeenth and early eighteenth century. This verse was requested by several Daily Express *readers who recalled it from primary school or Sunday school, and by Monica Groves from Manchester, who says her granny used to quote it when she and her sister started fighting.*

A GOOD PLAY
by Robert Louis Stevenson

We built a ship upon the stairs
All made of the back-bedroom chairs,
And filled it full of sofa pillows
To go a-sailing on the billows.

We took a saw and several nails,
And water in the nursery pails;
And Tom said, 'Let us also take
An apple and a slice of cake;' –
Which was enough for Tom and me
To go a-sailing on, till tea.

We sailed along for days and days,
And had the very best of plays;
But Tom fell out and hurt his knee,
So there was no one left but me.

To judge from letters to the Daily Express, *Robert Louis Stevenson is the best-forgotten poet in the English language. So many poems from his* Children's Garden Of Verses And Underwoods *have been requested, yet he is so often forgotten as the author.*

MARY HAD A LITTLE LAMB
by Sarah Josepha Hale

Mary had a little lamb,
Its fleece was white as snow;
And everywhere that Mary went,
The lamb was sure to go.

He followed her to school one day;
That was against the rule;
It made the children laugh and play;
To see a lamb at school.

And so the teacher turned it out,
But still it lingered near,
And waited patiently about
Till Mary did appear.

'Why does the lamb love Mary so?'
The eager children cry.
'Why, Mary loves the lamb, you know,'
The teacher did reply.

Sarah Josepha Hale (1788–1879)
*Sarah Josepha Hale of New Hampshire wrote this verse in 1830. It was based
on a true story of a girl called Mary Sawyer who brought her pet lamb to
school. It answers the question posed in an email by Mary Cunningham:
'Everyone knows the first verse of "Mary Had A Little Lamb", but what
happened next?'*

THE LAMPLIGHTER
by Robert Louis Stevenson

My tea is nearly ready and the sun has left the sky;
It's time to take the window to see Leerie going by;
For every night at teatime and before you take your seat,
With lantern and with ladder he comes posting up the street.

Now Tom would be a driver and Maria go to sea,
And my papa's a banker and as rich as he can be;
But I, when I am stronger and can choose what I'm to do,
O Leerie, I'll go round at night and light the lamps with you!

For we are very lucky, with a lamp before the door,
And Leerie stops to light it as he lights so many more;
And O! before you hurry by with ladder and with light;
O Leerie, see a little child and nod to him to-night!

This is a final verse by Stevenson to turn out the lights on this collection. May Jean from Enfield, Middlesex was prompted to ask for it when she saw the picture of a lamplighter in a copy of the Daily Express.

Index of first lines

Index of poets

About the Author

William Hartston has been writing for the *Daily Express* since 1998, contributing the daily Beachcomber column, as well as a variety of columns on useless information (including the daily Ten Things You Didn't Know About...), the Saturday Briefing page, and, of course, Forgotten Verse. He also contributes a number of the paper's puzzles, an expertise he attributes to a wasted youth. He has written extensively on the game of chess, and was British Chess Champion in 1973 and 1975.

Has this book brought back memories of any verse you may have learnt at school or come across later in life that you would like us to try to track down? We cannot promise to find it for you, or to reply to every letter and e-mail, but every request we receive is given consideration. Even when they are not published in the *Daily Express*, we often send personal replies, too – especially when prevented by copyright law from publishing them, or when the poems asked for have already appeared in the paper.

So if you do have any snippets of verse that need to be completed, just write to: Forgotten Verse, Daily Express, 10 Lower Thames Street, London EC3R 6EN, or e-mail william.hartston@express.co.uk and we'll do the best we can.

You will also find a Forgotten Verse section on our website at www.express.co.uk where, as well as offering a daily verse, we are building up a searchable archive of poems, including both those which have been published in the newspaper and many that have not.